BOOKS BY NICK LYONS

JONES VERY: SELECTED POEMS (editor)
THE SEASONABLE ANGLER
FISHERMAN'S BOUNTY (editor)
FISHING WIDOWS
THE SONY VISION
BRIGHT RIVERS
*CONFESSIONS OF A FLY FISHING
   ADDICT*
TROUT RIVER (text for photographs by
   Larry Madison)

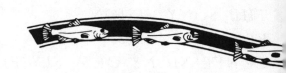

NICK LYONS

CONFESSIONS OF A FLY FISHING ADDICT

A FIRESIDE BOOK
PUBLISHED BY SIMON & SCHUSTER
NEW YORK   LONDON   TORONTO   SYDNEY   TOKYO

FIRESIDE
SIMON & SCHUSTER BUILDING
ROCKEFELLER CENTER
1230 AVENUE OF THE AMERICAS
NEW YORK, NEW YORK 10020

DESIGNED BY DIANE STEVENSON / SNAP·HAUS GRAPHICS

MANUFACTURED IN THE UNITED STATES OF AMERICA

1   2   3   4   5   6   7   8   9   10
    4   5   6   7   8   9   10   PBK.

LIBRARY OF CONGRESS CATALOGING IN PUBLICATION DATA

LYONS, NICK.
CONFESSIONS OF A FLY FISHING ADDICT.

"A FIRESIDE BOOK."
1.   FLY FISHING.   I. TITLE.   II. TITLE: CONFESSIONS
OF A FLY FISHING ADDICT.
SH456.L96 1989   799.1'2   88-36237

ISBN 0-671-68379-9
ISBN 0-671-67653-9   PBK.

All essays appeared originally as the "Seasonable Angler" column in *Fly Fisherman* magazine.

ACKNOWLEDGMENTS

I am extremely grateful to Don Zahner for giving me the last page of *Fly Fisherman* magazine many years ago, when I'd done little enough to earn it, and for much encouragement since then, including an invitation to "come back soon" when, eight years ago, my reservoir ran dry; and I am particularly grateful to John Randolph, the current editor and publisher of *Fly Fisherman*, for giving me back that spot when I was rested, and warmly supporting even my most bizarre imaginings. Janet Lonsdale's ideas on the ordering of these essays gave the book its final shape—and I am grateful to her for her perception and hard work on my behalf, and to Sol Skolnick and Sydny Miner for wanting to publish these confessions and ruminations of a fly fishing addict.

CONTENTS

PREFACE

Most of these essays are short. Fifteen years ago, when I began the "Seasonable Angler" column in *Fly Fisherman* magazine, from which all of the work in this book has been drawn, I feared the limitations of the short form. I wanted to write twice or more as much. I wanted to pour all of myself into each essay I wrote, and when I put together my first fishing books, I often combined columns or made one part of a larger whole, or I fully reworked them.

But the genre is compelling, and if you do a column long enough and think enough about its possibilities, it provides more than the leisure that Wordsworth claimed for one of his favorite short forms when he wrote, "Twas pastime to be bound / Within the sonnet's scanty plot of ground."

To me, the column of 1,200 to 1,400 words became enabling rather than restricting. Like the intimist painter, looking at a narrower world and finding more, I was able to explore otherwise minor but—at least to me—fascinating corners of the fly fisher's life and brain.

I learned to take one image, or several, and pursue it tenaciously. I could look at an hour's event on a private trout stream or consolidate all I know about salmon fishing. I could explore the anatomy of an addiction, *my* addiction, not especially to the broader world of fishing or to fishing for one species but to a specific method, fly fishing.

I found fly fishing sweet, compelling, at times humorous or at least whimsical, sometimes dead serious, concerned with a thousand skills to be learned and as many chances to fail. It has provided me with adventure, challenge, wonder, and a chance to build into my life a coherent discipline. It has been a foil against which I could hold the greater foibles of the world and a balm that helps me forget them, too.

Much of what I have written is about myself. I see now, and

quite clearly, looking back at these essays, that I have evolved into a very personal essayist, not a writer of articles or tracts or fiction. I have not illuminated many of the minor or major mysteries of fly fishing but have used myself and my passion as my chief subjects.

This is dangerous. It may imply that the writer finds nothing more interesting than his own ideas and his own navel. It may become solipsistic—or worse, merely boring. I hope my essays have not become this, and if they haven't, it may be because I don't think self-importance is one of my many sins; I have written about myself because, inevitably, he's whom I know best.

I have not been shy of making fun of myself and my pratfalls, but I have tried to keep in mind that the self-deprecation of a bumbler can not only be tedious but also a subtle plea for attention, even pity—and too easy a source of cheap humor. I bumble a lot, but I've also, over the years, learned a few things with fly rod in hand and I've tried to share these and I've tried to broach some serious issues.

I've fished too little at times—like too many of us—and too much at others; and I've tried to step back and reflect on what it all means. I can be opinionated at times... and weary of all opinions at others. I guess I've tried to bring to my writing my love of the "fish tale," my belief that story speaks louder than sermon; I've tried to affirm that the elusive soul of fly fishing is too often lost in the ambition and mechanics and competitiveness of much modern sport.

In this, my fifth book on fishing, I have chosen not to tinker and twist previous material into what I hoped would be a book but to leave the material alone, as it was written, as vignettes and essays and musings—perhaps because the genre, after my resistance to it, has at last seduced me.

I like it best this way and hope readers do, too.

Nick Lyons
New York City
Spring 1989

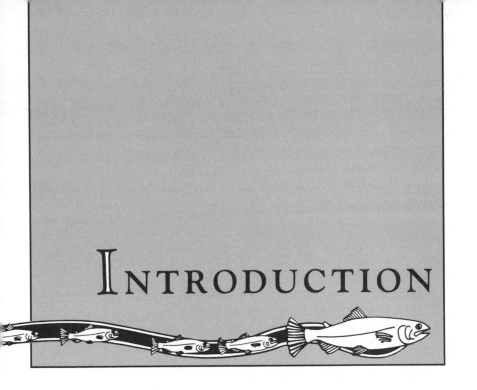

INTRODUCTION

FISH TALES

It's winter again and I have been fussing with all my flies and rods and reels, wondering (as I periodically do) why and how I have been gut-hooked by fly fishing. Surely the sheer wondrous technology is part of it, I think, looking at the immense variety of flies in my boxes, mumbling their names as if I were saying a mantra, running my fingers across the subtle tapers of rods, listening to the particular sound of a reel on which I wind a new fly line. When I squint, all the flies I've dumped into a shoe box look like so many jewels.

But my eyes look through the brilliance of the "things" of fly fishing to the stories—those odd, compelling, hilarious tales, in and out of print, that are so irresistible, and to the images and mind-pictures we record. "Had all Pens that go salmon fishing," wrote William McFarland in 1925, "devoted themselves to jotting down notes about why the big fish did not gobble a grasshopper, we should have lost many a page of sunshine, fresh air, and good fellowship, and reaped a crop of fireside Disko troops who thought like the fish."

In the best stories about fly fishing—by Norman Maclean, Roderick Haig-Brown, Robert Traver, Sparse Grey Hackle, William Humphrey, Howard Walden, and ten thousand others who tell them in camps and at lunch tables but do not write—we find the best clues to why some of us fish. Odd, funny things happen; there is mystery and suspense, challenge and discovery; the words have the warm colors of earth and water, not the jargon of the specialist; we meet real people, with warts and wit and maverick gestures; big fish are caught or lost; people say wild and spontaneous words; event becomes memory and sometimes, in the hands of a master, bleeds into art.

Such is surely the case with Sparse's story "Murder," about a man who catches a gigantic trout while trying to escape the doldrums of the Depression—and discovers that even fishing won't let him escape the harried world of affairs (though I've found it a good start), and Howard Walden's "When All the World Was Young," about a boy becoming a man, and William Humphrey's hilarious dissection of days (and nights) in a Scottish salmon-fishing hotel, *The Spawning Run.*

Many of the best fish tales only begin with the fish. There is a scene in Maclean's *A River Runs Through It* in which the narrator and his brother go looking for a pal who has taken a local lady of low repute along on the fishing trip, and downriver. The pal has taken her way downriver. The lady's name is Old Rawhide. The men turn a bend and come upon an odd sight in the middle of the Big Blackfoot River. "Maybe it's a bear," says the narrator. "That's no bear," Paul says. They study the sandbar. Maybe it's two bears. "Bear, hell," Paul says when they get closer. "It's a bare ass." "Two bare asses," says the narrator, and reports: "You have never really seen an ass until you have seen two sunburned asses on a sandbar in the middle of a river. Nearly all the rest of the body seems to have evaporated. The body is a large red ass about to blister, with hair on one end of it for a head and feet attached to the other end for legs. By tonight it will run a fever." And a page later he adds: "I never again threw a line in this hole, which I came to regard as a kind of wild game sanctuary."

Sometimes a fish tale is a brief image, a moment, a few words: an angler I'd met for the first time, telling me about a gigantic rainbow trout he'd been pursuing all morning on Bonefish

Flats of the Henry's Fork with #22 midge pupae. The man's eyes, half-crazy, were nearly out of his skull. Or my marvelously fanatic French friend, Pierre, breaking his rod, then his line, losing a record 180-pound tarpon at the boat, and leaping onto it, straddling the thing like the cowboy pilot straddling the bomb in *Dr. Strangelove*. Or me, sinking slowly into the mud (on which I guess I thought I could walk), right up to my tweed jacket, on a gentle British chalkstream, in front of some perfectly bewildered British friends who'd never dreamed they'd see such a sight on their genteel waters.

Fish tales can occur anywhere, even in the bowels of cities, where some of us spend a few too many of our days. I once sent a young, rather shy English friend, on his first trip to America, to see Jim Deren, the late proprietor of the Angler's Roost in New York City, about buying a dozen flies for a weekend in the Catskills. Jimmy was scrunched behind his counter in that tiny, crowded, inimitable shop, and when Neil introduced himself, with quiet British courtesy, he growled: "I can tell from that accent that you're from across the pond—from over there. Well, mister, we use small flies here, too." And he reached under the counter and brought up a cupped hand. "Have you ever used flies *this* small?"

Neil looked into the hand. There was only pure pink palm. He thought this might be some sort of American joke he didn't understand and said, "Well, they're pretty small—but no smaller, old sport, than the ones I use." And Neil put *his* hand into his pocket and brought it out empty, too. Later he told me in perfect wonderment: "Nick, we talked about those empty hands for a full twenty minutes, and then I asked for some Hendricksons, like you told me, and he tried to sell me some air, and I walked out of the place in shock and never bought a thing."

The first plumes of skunk cabbage out of the brown earth; the spectral light and delicate green of the willows in April; Hendricksons popping out and then floating downriver like little sailboats on the Willowemoc; a trout tipping up ever so slowly for a drift of spinners; collecting scraps of sable and fox with Justin from the side streets off Seventh Avenue in June, which (converted into trout flies) we reckoned had a street value of twenty-eight million dollars; bleak days when not a fish showed; a day on the

Beaverkill when every trout in the river went bananas; Lee Wulff talking quietly about his pioneering days of flying and salmon fishing in Newfoundland, buzzing the river valleys to spook schools of salmon and thus locate them; a Connecticut lake at daybreak, when largemouth bass crashed up out of the mists for hair bugs as big as bats, which Larry and I threw at them—their rises less like a trout poking its snout up than like a garbage can being chucked into the lake; the Delaware at dusk, when the sun slanted silver and red down the alley of the river, distances blurred, a certain sweet chill entered the air, the surface was suddenly pocked with a dozen rising trout, and Ed took a gigantic brown that for twenty minutes he thought must be a shad hooked in the tail; the flow of the lower Neversink in my ears and against my body; the deep, happy ache in my shoulders after a long day of casting; my first sight of a landlocked salmon, skyrocketing into the air, a gash of silver; a letter from a friend out West, describing the pursuit and capture of a twenty-four-inch brown—with the postscript that the one he was *really* after could have eaten the one he'd quickly traced for me on newsprint; a brown with shoulders angling up from beneath the willow on the Beaverhead, its mouth fearsome, like a dog's, to take a tiny Elk Hair Caddis—these and a thousand other moments and images, remembered as I fuss with tackle in the dead of winter, are the stuff of fly fishing for me, and perhaps some of the mysterious "why" of it.

There is some lunacy in it all—and some playing Huck Finn, to regain our childhood. But that lunacy and those images are specks of sand that, like the sand in an oyster, become a fisherman's pearls. Some are funny jewels, some sad, and some touch our hearts. All are part of the great storehouse of memories and tales that make up a fisherman's quirky and crammed brain, keeping us gut-hooked from one season through the long gray winters until another season starts. In the end, the fisherman avoids the glitz of the new, the quagmire of too many innovations and new techniques, and this competitive monster The Fishing Contest, and returns to the simple, lovely pleasures of the sport itself: days filled with "sunshine, fresh air, and good fellowship," and sometimes a bit of raw hide, and a pursuit that never quite ends, and images and words that brighten our often darkened spirits.

It is late winter now and I have grown restless, grumpy, sour. I am beginning to count days until the season opens again. I fiddle with my rods and reels and flies, put away the books, check my waders for leaks, and then take out all the jewels that are my memories, and, silently, gloat over them.

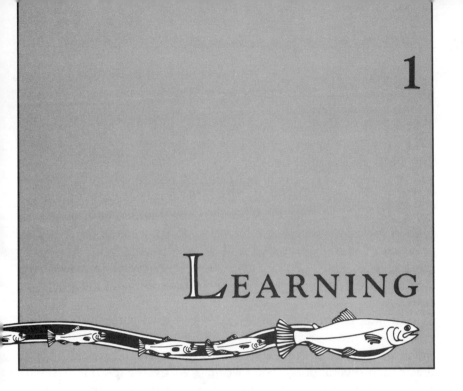

1

LEARNING

CONFESSIONS OF AN EARLY WORMER

When I was fifteen and we lived in Brooklyn and all the other guys were off hunting girls, I would often sneak out of my house on a muggy late-March evening, wearing sneakers and carrying a flashlight and coffee can. On the corner of Bedford Avenue and Avenue J, I would meet my friend Mort, and the two of us, with great bounding strides, would head without a word for the huge abandoned house several blocks away, its windows dark, a "For Sale" sign stuck prominently into the front lawn. And among the high clumps of untended grass, only barely green, our hearts would quicken and we would begin to hunt worms.

More snake than worm, these night crawlers were long, floppy, gooey things, often stretched out to six or seven inches on their spawning crawl. We would shine the light so that only its edge illuminated the shiny back of a worm, then plunge quickly to catch one where it left the earth, pinning it lightly, firmly, then easing it up out of its hole. Later we learned to put red paper over the faces of our flashlights, and we could shine the dimmer light directly on these night crawlers without their moving. We often caught the old hermaphrodites at it, quite passionately joined together at the necks, and now and again Mort or I would say, in a loud whisper, "Double," and we'd display two with as much pride as a wing-shooter after his feat.

We were always quick and intent about our business. We had to be. More than twenty minutes on any lawn usually meant the cops. We had "safe" lawns, where we could linger, and some well-tended lawns whose owners thought we were madmen, burglars, or worse. Carefully trimmed and watered lawns were usually the most fecund, and one old lady, whose immaculate lawn was irresistible, often sat shotgun so we "beastly boys" wouldn't pinch *her* worms.

It was a strange, mystical rite—this catching of night crawlers on moist spring nights—and we somehow took almost as much pleasure in it as we did in fishing. Rarely did we return with fewer than several dozen good worms. We even experimented with scores of different materials in which to store the bait—from cut newspaper to grass—and finally settled on sphagnum moss, which we bought in vast quantities from a dealer in Arkansas. We packed the moss and worms in shoe boxes, and I, who had an understanding mother, kept them in the vegetable section of my refrigerator.

They were our foremost baits for trout, these snakelike night crawlers, and for several years we caught all our early-season trout on them. Though by May, when the water was low and clear, we switched to small garden worms—a firmer, more compact creature—all our April fishing was done with these preposterous monsters. And we caught fish. Big two- and even three-pound holdover brown trout, from hard-fished public waters, fell to our ungainly rigs.

We gave them up not for flies but for spinning lures, and spent the last few years of our teens becoming lethal with this new tool that enabled you to flip a $\frac{1}{16}$-ounce spinner forty feet, to the base of a fallen tree, and retrieve it with subtle fluttering.

Spinning taught me much that I've put to good use when streamer fishing—but probably condemned me to a floppy casting wrist for life; only years of careful fly casting have burned away the haste, the impatience, the nervous movement spinning taught me so well. None of my previous fishing prepared me for the challenge of the dry fly, and only recently have I begun to appreciate how much I learned about wet-fly and nymph fishing from my early worming.

At first we fished worms on long, unwieldy telescopic fly rods. We did not so much cast as heave or lope the rig out—a big night crawler hooked lightly in its orange band with a #8 Eagle Claw hook, then ten inches of leader, then as much split shot as we needed to get the thing where we wanted it. We used four of the biggest shot in the Big Bend Pool, merely one in the deep Swamp Pool, none in several slow glides where we'd fish it straight upstream and follow its progress down with the tip of the rod. On Opening Day, we used the most primitive methods and fished the deepest, slowest pools, smack in the middle, dead still, right on the bottom. On warmer days, we'd fish the head of a pool, drifting a worm from the riffle down into the center or sides—still as deep as possible. And even with "bugs" hatching all around us and trout rising with bacchanalian slurps, we fished—and caught fish— with worms. We'd use the smallest worms then, the lightest leaders; we'd fish shallow runs or riffles, or wherever we saw fish rising. We fished upstream and watched the worm come back toward us, a few inches beneath the surface—and often enough we'd see one of the better trout cease all that peanut grabbing and head for a good, decent munch of worm.

How did all this early worming affect a closet fly fisherman?

I suppose at first it merely humiliated me to have done it. I mentioned it not at all, could find no connection between it and the dry-fly fishing I now did—except that I had always caught a lot of fish on worms.

But then I realized that there was a certain "pool" of streamlore I had developed before I caught any fish, even on worms—a knowledge of where, at a particular time of the year and day, fish would be; a sense of what will frighten them; an inkling of what they would eat and under what circumstances they would take it. I had begun to learn this kind of lore while worming. Before long, I learned that trout were rarely taken in open, exposed water; they wanted protection from the heavy flow, and from predators, and they wanted a spot where vulnerable food would come to them.

Pockets behind rocks, with their broken water and eddies, were ideal: here the trout had protection and had ready access to food caught and stunned and perhaps eddying in the broken water.

After the holocaust of Opening Day, our most regular success came from fishing these spots, what Al Troth calls the supermarkets of the river, with immense care. We learned that we could not drop a worm smack in the middle of such a pocket because the turbulence would scoot it right out and into the main flow; we had to get the worm slightly upstream first, then give enough slack so the bait would sink to the proper depth, then manipulate the rod in such cunning ways that the bait would remain in the pockets. Bends in the rivers created undercut banks and greater water depth, and we also took fish by working a worm slowly, naturally, into their depths.

Naturally.

That, I think, is the key word. Mort used to say, when a dumb hatchery fish took a quickly retrieved worm: "Mistook that one for a worm swimming upstream." And we'd continue the conceit with references to "hatches" of upstream-swimming worms and other unnatural absurdities. No. The tough fish, the good-sized fish, were only caught when you fished the worm naturally. And since a worm does not usually swim upstream, or hang suspended from a leader on the bottom of a river, *natural* meant dead drift: with the worm cast upstream, gaining a bit of depth as it moved down, without encumbrance, tumbling as close to the bottom as possible.

We learned to hold the rod forward and then bring it downstream as the worm came toward and past us. We learned to see the telltale twitch of line or leader, the wink of white underwater when a trout's mouth opened. We learned to manipulate the bait to the depth at which the fish were; we learned to judge currents and eddies in the process. We learned holding water and feeding lanes and how to use our eyes and hands, and we learned the absolute need for quick, light strikes.

Though we didn't know it, we were beginning to learn how to fish the nymph.

Now and again, when I hear someone tell me how they learned to fly fish when they were five or ten or twelve, I get a touch of envy, a sense of regret, a feeling that all of my green years, when my feelings and passions were freshest, might have been better spent. As I look back, I was from the beginning fated to be a fly fisherman: everything I love about fishing pointed me in that direction. Now and again, when I think back on my early years, I regret I did not find fly fishing sooner.

But lately, especially in late March, when Mort and I first went forth with flashlight and coffee can, I remember the lowly worm: the moist nights on which we hunted them, the engaging *peck-peck-peck* when a fish took one, the whole ritual of worm fishing. But beyond all that, beyond that world to which I cannot return, I am grateful to the worm. It was a damned good teacher.

HOMAGE À BLUEGILLS— AND PUMPKINSEEDS, TOO

Durocher once said of Eddie Stanky: "He can't run, he can't field, and he can't hit, but he's the best player on the Dodgers." It could be said of bluegills and pumpkinseeds that they run to no size, can be caught in dreary field ponds, and will hit even ciga-rette butts—but I won't say it.

They are the harlequins of kids' hearts, a grand and generous fish, a whiff of youth for many a middle-aged trout snob.

Me, for instance.

Lepomis machrochirus—it belies the lovely simplicity of the bluegill to drape it in Latin; pumpkinseed, *Lepomis gibbosus*, of the bright orange belly, with shimmering green-blue sides and that prickly dorsal you must smooth and lock back with a thrust of your palm: low on the pecking order, high in hearts.

They were the first fish I caught on a fly, the first I caught by *any* method, and in my dotage, when the fly comes no longer lightly to the rise, I hope some good soul will wheel me to the bank of a weedy field pond with lots of pancake-sized spawning nests in view, so I can slap my Bumble Bee down while shuffling slowly through senility and off this mortal coil. Often enough, the fly comes not light even now—and a good substitute for throwing myself upon a sword when I've botched the trout game is surely to let the *Lepomis* massage my ego a bit with their ready antics.

If only they weren't so small, I used to moan when I first caught them in South Lake and in the lake runoff (where they were positively stunted). The cork bobber, threaded through, would begin a spritely jig, then dart down at an angle; I'd yank, and there it was, flopping in the boat a second later—four inches of flopping blue, green, and orange, maybe five. One didn't particularly have to be a big-fish fisherman to desire more for one's cranelike wait: they were midgets; they were—no doubt about it—a one-yank fish.

When I was sent, rather against my will, to a gloomy boarding school in Peekskill, bluegills and pumpkinseeds were my salvation. I credit them with no less. I was five, then six, then seven, then eight there—and they yanked me through. For all the gray of grayness, for all the chest-wracking loneliness I felt in that old Victorian spookhouse of a school, the little Ice Pond—a couple of acres of it—was green and live and generous. Though quite alone, I was never once lonely there. I can look intently at one photograph taken of me, knee-deep in that muddy pond, in short pants and a sailor's blouse, holding a crooked bark-stripped poplar pole, and there is no touch of loneliness on the face. The eyes are intent, awake, as if through the pole and cheap green line I am plugged into some life current.

It was only a muddy pond with no current, a big basin of tepid water near a highway, this Ice Pond, but it was the home of harlequins. I learned to wait and watch, to stalk with some caution, to *think* underwater. Mostly I caught bluegills, fewer and bigger than those at South Lake, and a few bright, mature pumpkinseeds that circled with tough tugs and had to be eased, not yanked, from their element. On a Saturday afternoon in May, when others went with their guests, I could stand there hour after hour, my toes curled into the mud, my corn-kernel can of dug worms on a nearby rock, my eyes unflinchingly locked to the cork bobber.

And so, on bluegills and pumpkinseeds, the hook was set deep, into the marrow and into the affections—and when the hook grew feathers, the fish were still there, still as happily accommodating. (I only wish my own children had come to fishing on them, for their trout days have been long and often fishless and frustrating.)

I was seventeen or eighteen when I bought my first fly rod for fly fishing; I'd had a telescopic steel rod first—after the cut or cane poles—then a twelve-buck Heddon bamboo that broke on a foul-hooked ten-pound carp, then an array of spinning rods with which I learned to perform prodigious feats. But I never used flies with those first fly rods, only bait. That summer in my late teens, while waiting on tables at a summer camp, I earned enough to buy an eight-foot glass fly rod, a dozen cheap, snelled flies, and a level C flyline and spool of level leader. I had been watching, with increasing awe, the fly fishermen who plied their elusive art on afternoons when I was about to leave the East or West Branch of the Croton. They seemed no less than an advanced stage of evolution; there was grace and delicacy in what they did. Better, they never snagged bottom—and they *did* catch fish when even I, the master of worm and spinner, could not.

So I bought the ill-matched mishmash of gear that summer, and since Ellis Pond was handy and I had my evenings free, I'd head off beyond the docks to a weedy flat near the bend of the shore and flail away. No one taught me—which showed. (And still does.) I put backcasts into rocks and shrubs, slapped the water to a thick foam, tangled myself in my level C flyline—and caught bluegills.

Did I catch bluegills!

That ragged #8 Bumble Bee could take thirty in an evening. Whipping and waving, I'd get the fly a few feet beyond my nose, down on the water like a tossed rock, and they'd riot for it. Against the soft bend of the rod, they couldn't be yanked, and I learned finger positions for drawing in line, getting it back on the reel, keeping it from tangling at my feet. We educated each other, those bluegills and I: by late August, they were warier, I was defter.

Not deft enough for trout, not nearly so—but better. Good enough to cast, say, twenty-five feet. Good enough to jiggle the fly, twitch it just right, so it brought that pinched swirl that let me know a fish had taken the slightly sunken, battered Bee.

•   •   •

Now and then the chance comes to taste a food you loved as a child—fresh wild strawberries, perhaps, or tart blackberries from a thorny bush. Berries with memories. Bill Humphrey and I had found his local creeks dead as trapped mice one hot June afternoon, and he whisked me up to a little weedy pond on a neighbor's land. It was rarely fished. It was quite choked already with lily pads and long, high weed. It was perhaps fifty yards all the way around. But what fat bluegills it had, and how readily they came to tiny popping bugs that evening! And what simple good fun we had, mingled with memories, as we stalked through the high grasses along the shore. We'd cast one of those six-for-a-buck poppers out, twitch it, let it sit, twitch it again. A midget would tap the thing, *splat-splat*, then a big gulp-rise and a plump bluegill was on, circling at right angles against the tug of the line, tugging with its jerky tugs, twice its weight in pluck.

They were fat, but if only they were still a *little* larger, I thought.

And then, last week, Thom Green called me from Tulsa. He is a big-fish fisherman of the first water. He takes big lake rainbows on his big brown Leech; record white bass; cutthroats the size of your arm. He casts his shooting-head a hundred feet and prowls big waters for big fish. There was this pond in Utah, he said.

Did it hold rainbows, big browns?

Nope.

Fat smallmouths, maybe?

Bluegills.

Bluegills?

"Well," he said, "I'd heard about it, and the reports told of bluegills up to a pound, pound and a half."

"Those're big bluegills."

"But then I was working in that area last fall and got to speak to the local conservation officer. When I asked him about the pond, he said, 'Would you believe two to *three* pounds?'"

"The conservation officer said that?"

"Can you go this summer, Nick?"

"To Utah? For bluegills?" I'd rather been working my mind into a salmon mood, or perhaps the Madison during stone-fly time. I had Henrys Fork on the brain—and the East Branch, the Firehole, and dusk hatches in long Montana evenings.

"The man said, 'Would you believe two to *three* pounds?'"

"But that's two thousand miles..."

"On popping bugs. *Three-pound bluegills.*"

Lepomis machrochirus monstruosus! Wouldn't dreams of *those* enliven my dotage!

"Will you go?"

"I'm already there," I said.

THE CASTING PERPLEX

That March, while I was in college, I often trotted over to the Palestra with fly rod in hand. The basketball season was over, mounds of sooty snow still spotted the street corners of Philadelphia, and I was mad for the trout season to begin.

I had not really started to fly fish yet, but the tool—a cream-white Shakespeare fiberglass rod—intrigued me. I had used it for bait-fishing the previous spring and with flies, for bluegill. When the season opened that year, I was determined to try fly fishing for trout.

My prospects were discouraging. The mismatched level line was too light for the stiff rod and would not work it. I snapped the thing back and forth like a bullwhip. The line came back too slow, my loops were ludicrously wide or else got tangled in their absurdities, and I jerked my rod hand around so much I nearly ruined it for spinning.

I was crazy for distance. Standing at midcourt, I wanted to wing the thing far beneath the backboard and into the stands. The harder I tried the more I flopped. I could not do it.

On short casts—very short casts—I wasn't nearly so helpless. With no more than twenty feet out, I almost thought I could manage this madness. My barbless hook dropped with unerring accuracy on the foul line. But at thirty feet I ached for a spinning rod, at which I was a master.

I fumbled here and there, split time with other fishing tools, and then, some years later—without prompting, without a coach, and without more than a fool's sense of what I was doing—committed myself the whole hog to the long rod. And then, to do what I wanted to do, to reach that eddy near the far bank or get a drag-free float through the riffle, I began to take my casting with a terrible seriousness.

I began matching my line to my rod. This proved one of my wiser decisions. I used a tapered line: also not a bad idea. I considered the size and taper of my leader and without too much tinkering, found that it was not inevitable that a leader should jerk and hook and then lie like a halfmoon on the surface. I learned that less could indeed be more: by firming up my wrist, keeping my casting arm closer to the vertical, and allowing the line to work the rod, I cast farther and with far less energy. Gone, suddenly, was the feverish bullwhip mentality; gone, too, were the maddening tangles and loss of control. Phil Wright taught me to control the line with my line hand and then, to my astonishment, got me to do the double-haul in fifteen minutes one afternoon—well, my unique version of that valuable cast.

So I began to get the business done a bit better, to reach the line a bit to the left or right when needed, to cast sidearm or backhand when I had to, to send the fly out far enough to get a fish or two now and then when they were beyond what I'd thought was my limit, and to roll out a creditable cast or two under branches. Except to myself, in giddy moments, I had few pretensions. I had begun to see what magic others could wreak with the fly rod; I knew my limitations. And I had other fishing interests to fly: there were new kinds of streamcraft, a growing interest in still waters, entomology, tackle tinkering of a rudimentary stripe, tying, improving my eyesight and hindsight.

But you can't do a thing at all unless you can cast: it's that fundamental. And now and then, watching one of the masters in motion, I had an itch to become truly dazzling with the tool.

But they all did it so differently.

Art Flick, moving with astonishing speed and purpose, had his fly on the water five times more than anyone I'd seen. He flicked his fly here and there, followed it, lifted, cast again, had his fly working for him while I dawdled. But when I went fast, I fumbled again.

I watched in wonder when Ed Van Put laid out a long, lazy

line and then watched in dismay as my line, at twice his speed, crashed to the surface behind me.

When I saw Lee Wulff put his index finger up on the cork handle and cast eighty feet without much more effort than I used to breathe, I immediately tried this and found I forced the line too hard and it did whacky things.

I only saw a movie of Lefty Kreh, but when I tried for his distance, I was the complete tangler again. What authority and ease he had. And just when I thought I'd learned something about casting, I knew I knew nothing.

I knew it would take me twenty years, fishing every day, to fish the way Doug Swisher did that day on the Big Hole, dancing his line, attacking the river with deft skill. And if it took the balanced, classic casts that Schwiebert made that day on the Grimsa to catch salmon, I'd have to go back to chub on the short line. He was quite marvelously fine.

Thom Green laid out 120 feet of line on Henrys Lake, with a shooting head, and I watched as he drew his rod arm back, almost parallel to the water, then, with his whole body, winged it forward. The line went out and out, and then the leader turned over with a last little flip and I bought myself a shooting head for Christmas. With it, with a great deal of effort, I could cast almost as far as I could with a standard shooting taper.

Beyond my pleasure in watching all these men at work—and once, Joan Wulff make it all look ludicrously easy—I was perplexed. Was there a *proper* way to cast? I didn't have to be particularly perceptive to notice that each of these fly casters was different. Each had, what we call in stuffy English departments, a style of his or her own. *Style est l'homme.* Flick flicked and Van Put putted slowly: they both got the work done. Bob Buckmaster cast as if he were driving a nail, with sharp *thwack, thwacks*, and Pierre Affre (that afternoon at Riverside Park) cast like a tooled machine, all in a rush of frightening motion, his rod going back far farther than even Thom Green's, the line no more than four feet off the ground, and then the awesome shoot.

I was baffled, perplexed.

I had a sincere desire to improve myself and thought I *had* been improving myself, but these birds were all so different. One proved his theories with the help of an orthopedic hand doctor;

another used a classical exemplum, such as Steve Rajeff; others recommended wristbands, books under the elbow, and whatnot else. Worse, with my ear not particularly flush to the ground, I began to hear rumblings of backbiting and rivalry. "What does Swisher know about casting?" "Do you really call Schwiebert a caster?"

Yes, Virginia, I do. And Swisher knows awfully well whereof he speaks. So do the others. Some are professional coaches and greatly skillful at it. Had I the time or money I could invest it in worse efforts than a casting clinic with the Wulffs or with Swisher. They'd make anyone better.

Someone recently wrote to this magazine saying that his son could tell wines like Ernest Schwiebert and cast like Nick Lyons. This is no lie. You can ask the editors. He couldn't have mixed us up because I can't tell a Riesling from a Margaux. And I read his sentence as a compliment. But the man must be a lunatic. No one would *boast* that he or anyone he knew cast like me.

How does Nick Lyons cast?

I could answer, with false modesty: painfully, with limited success, rarely reaching the foul line. But though no showman, I'm better than that, though it's less fun to say so.

How do I cast?

Like Nick Lyons. I cast my own way. I use my wrist a bit too much, my backcast often goes too high, I have been known to slap the water (fore and aft), my puddle cast too often collapses like a mess of spaghetti. But most of the time I get the business done—each year a bit more handily.

Isn't that what it's all about?

JUST A CAST AWAY

"I'm a lousy caster," the guy shouted, smiling broadly, "but I sure have a lot of fun."

Since I'd heard the same sentiment from my own lips, I felt I'd earned the right to mumble: "I'm a better caster than I was, and I have more fun than I did."

The guy was flailing away on the Yellowstone in the Park, having as much fun as a clown; the fish were out there, rising by the hundreds, just a cast away, but he was catching nothing. How could he? He slapped the water only a bit less on his backcast than he did on his front cast. His high loops, buffeted merrily by the wind, dropped the line fifteen feet short or to the left of the rising fish to which he cast. His wrist, flopping back and forth, was a speeded-up metronome. Twice his fly actually floated over the fish, but at a gallop—for his cast those times had been *too* accurate, without slack to eat possible drag. Three times he had to cut a cast fly out of his vest or shirt, once by taking his vest off, losing a fly box in the process, and nearly losing his footing, which is easy enough in the Yellowstone. I feared for an eye or a cheek or an earlobe.

And through it all, thousands of those generous Yellowstone cutthroats kept tipping up and feeding safely on a perfectly splendid and generous hatch of tan caddis, perfectly safe from this poor bumbler.

Had he not been happy as a pig in mud, I'd have waded out and shook him by the shoulders for a full minute. Why so many of us fly fishermen have felt, for so long, comfortable with our incompetence, I don't know—unless it's because when we try to learn and can't, we feel like three-thumbed imbeciles—so we don't try and are insulated from possible failure. Or perhaps we think of fly fishing as merely a "poetic" leisure sport, and of practice as too much like work.

Anyway, I'd been where this guy was. A lot of times.

I'd stood in the same river during the same hatch—and caught nothing. Funny as that genial bumbler looked, on the river in front of me and in my memories, I turned my back on him in a few moments; I'd never enjoyed being there, though I had liked to write about it, and I soon found the scene too painful.

On the drive out of the Park I remembered the sudden change from frustration to pleasure after Phil Wright taught me the double-haul; I could not only cast farther but with more control; I gained line-hand control when I'd thought you only cast with your right hand. I remembered the day on a Madison River float when Glenn West taught me to cast lower and

harder into the wind, and a particular moment on a small secluded pond when I saw something in Craig Mathews' casting
that helped me from then on to lay down a dry fly more gently.
I remembered the authority and power I'd seen in casting demonstrations by Steve Rajeff and Lefty Kreh and Mel Krieger and
Joan Wulff, the fluid strength and control and purpose in their
casts.

Fly fishing is composed of many interrelated skills: poor approach will spook your quarry before you can strip line off your
reel for the first time; too thick a leader will give a fish acute
anxiety, and using too heavy a line for particular water will put a
fish on a fast just as fast; the wrong fly—because of size or pattern
or design—will draw no rise, no matter how brilliant the cast. But
all other things being proper, you *must* cast well or you will catch
few fish. And casting well—whatever you have been promised—
ain't easy: it is the development of skills that will meet a couple of
thousand special fishing situations, and that takes more than an
hour.

Perhaps a fish is rising seventy feet away and cannot be ap-
proached closer—and you can only cast an honest sixty; or the
wind is from the right and you don't know how to use a backhand
cast; or you must hook to the left, or to the right, or get decent
S-curves into your line if you want to avoid drag on a particular
stretch of river; or you want to throw an especially heavy bass bug
or a #24 Trico on a twenty-foot leader.

You are finally *there,* in the right place at the right time; you
even have the perfect imitation of a *dorothea,* the fish's lunch. The
fish is only a cast away . . . and that's too far.

Those situations occur far more frequently than I'm willing to
admit.

I was fishing not long ago on a very shallow, very clear river
with very large and very skittery trout. The fellow I was fishing
with knew the river well, and I'd heard he was a truly great caster
—though no hard chances had come his way that day.

We came around a back bend and together looked up a
hundred-foot stretch of this water—narrow here, with a glassy
surface, little cover, none of the water more than a couple of feet
deep. As we stood beside each other, scanning the water for a
feeding fish, I saw at once how difficult this river was. The shal-

low water meant that the fish had a tiny cone of vision and a fly would have to float within inches of their lies if they were even to see it. There were no trees, nothing to cast shadows, so the full light of a bright blue sky was over the water—and these fish suffered most from airborne predators; so anything moving, such as a fly line, would scare them silly. I took a step and the ripples and little waves went out thirty-five feet ahead of me. I moved an arm and a fish from the far bank darted madly upstream.

Ah, the sweet mad toughness of it.

We stood for five or ten minutes, still as poles, scanning the surface for a dorsal, a wake, a delicate rise. There were none. Then, where the current hit off a point seventy-five feet upstream and made a slight but discernible ten-foot foam line, a fish came up with authority. There were a few #18 Pale Morning Duns on the water, and they must have been what had brought this fellow up. Up he'd come, every minute or so—not much more frequently than that. I imagined him a wise old dog of a trout, fat and territorial, not given to feeding binges anymore, having a sweet tooth for these little sulfur bonbons. The way it lolled just under the surface, its dorsal out, and the steady, heavy way it moved, suggested it might be one of the larger fish in a river not known for its pikers.

I could not even contemplate the cast necessary to take such a fish. I knew just enough to know I'd botch it. You could not cast directly over the fish or it would surely bolt for safety. If you cast to the right and hooked the line left, the bulk of the line would fall on the shore. If you cast too roughly, by millimeters, no matter where the fly landed the fish would vanish. False casts would be disastrous. The water dropped off toward the left, and some brush there would make all but some brand of steeple cast impossible from that side—and such a cast inevitably would come down too hard. And you'd get one cast, no more: the water was too thin, the fish were too wary—like a Japanese brush painter, you'd have to catch it just right on the first try or try again some other time.

Five years ago I wouldn't have thought twice about turning such a fish over to the better fisherman. Now I thought twice and then decided to turn it over. I was a better caster now but not nearly good enough for this situation.

My friend grunted and said all right he'd try it, and then he stripped off a great number of coils of line, hesitated, and (without a false cast) made the most astonishing cast I've ever seen. I've always valued trout rivers precisely because they're so far from the modern technological world—but I'd have welcomed an instant replay this time. As best I can reconstruct what happened—and I have replayed it a dozen times—he cast partially *underhand* (so that the line never rose more than a foot off the surface of the water, and thus could be laid down lightly), he cast far to the *left*, across stream (so the line never came near the fish); and then he hooked the line back to the right, so that the fly flipped up near the spit of land, several feet above the fish, caught the little line of current exactly, and came down over the place where the rise-form had been just a minute before. I should add that there was a brisk downstream wind against us and that the cast was comfortably seventy-five to eighty feet.

It was a magical moment.

I let out an immense gasp of air.

And the fish came up as nice as you please and took the fly.

Until I can cast eighty or ninety feet (honest count) with one false cast, lay my fly down like down on a dime, with an S-curve or a triple air-mend or a left hook, or whatever else is needed, I guess I'll keep trying. Fishing may not be a spectator sport, but I sure had fun watching that cast. Being able to make it myself would have been even more fun.

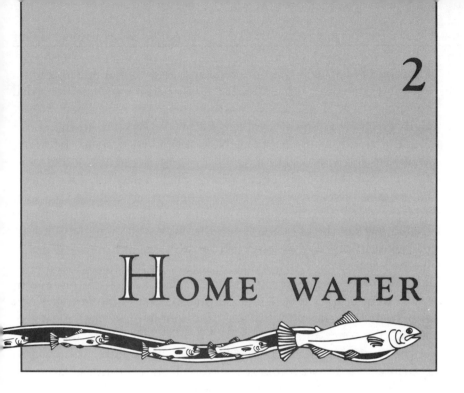

2

HOME WATER

HALCYON NIGHT

All things come to he who waits, some wistful philosopher once said. But I never believed such bilge. Poetic justice is rare, and it usually comes to the wrong people. Still one keeps trying to improve one's casting, one's knowledge of bugs, one's knots, and one's streamlore. And one hopes—blindly, irrationally.

One season gave immense promise of halcyon days and promptly showed its true drab colors. Reports from ten different sources told me that the East Branch was hot—so I trooped the three hours out of New York City to see for myself. I found the water painfully low, the few fish rising to be chub—a species of which I am, sadly, a master. Then I knocked around the Catskills with Bill Kelly and Len Wright, in pursuit of a smoky-blue phantom called the shad. Kelly, who was a senior biologist in the area and is a superb fisherman, had caught thousands of them. Len, who's no slouch, had never tried for them. Kelly promised us a sackful; we even began to divvy up the roe—those two wise birds insisting it tasted awful and I should give them my share. We tried

Hickory Pool, then stood on a downstream bridge and spotted a dozen of the smoky-blue wraiths, then tried for those, then tried the main river. I got a few taps but they may have been stones. Kelly got hooked up once, but it was on the bottom. In the end, I found myself four hours out of New York City, tired to the bone, and we'd caught not a thing.

Do not think I am complaining. Such a day, filled with good banter and pleasant talk, with the bright rivers waking your eyes and the earth and trees going green everywhere, is surely better than a poke in the eye or a day in the city.

Still, it's nice to catch a fish or two now and then. And that spring I waited patiently, wistfully, for such a rare occurence.

With no particular expectation of doing much of that catching, I went upstate with Knox Burger later that same spring. Knox is a literary agent who believes in "honest prose and nerves of steel." I've seen him wear a T-shirt displaying that message. I warned him that he might need a barrel of the latter if he was to get through a day with me, the way my luck was running lately.

But it was a gorgeous early June morning, and I kept thinking of George Herbert's lovely lines:

> Sweet day, so cool, so calm, so bright,
> The bridal of the earth and sky;

which Walton quotes, too, probably on a similar day. Perhaps there are a dozen of them in the spring—days that have a certain sweetness, that seem suspended, delicately, out of time entirely. There were lacy buds, yellow-green, on the trees; the air was a blend of sunwarmth and windcool, and the elements were so happily commingled that you could not tell which was the undertaste, which would predominate, if one had to do that.

We'd chosen a corner of the Catskills that gets less traffic than the big Beaverkill or one of the Delaware stems, wanting matters quieter, more private, after a crowded week. We had the river to ourselves and the day showed every promise of being a pleasant one.

Any beautiful river has a lien on my soul. This one, smaller and more intimate than most, has a large lien. It's nearer the origin of things, less traveled; it has a full complement of runs, riffles, bends, and pools; it can be extremely generous—and I have walked away from it blanked and beaten.

Knox hadn't fished it and I hoped—as we all hope when we take a good friend out—that it would be a strong day. I wanted him to catch fish more than I wanted to catch fish, and I wanted to catch fish very much, indeed.

We started in the upper section, where the water is thinner, quicker. With no flies showing, I thought we might pound up a few fish on a Gray Fox Variant or Hair-Wing Coachman. But the fishing was slow. Perhaps the water was a bit too low and clear; perhaps the sun was a bit too bright on the riffles; perhaps the trout wanted their salami sandwiches fished to them under the surface. But we kept working the dry fly upstream all afternoon, one of us catching up to the other, leapfrogging, moving at a leisurely pace, catching between us a couple of small browns, seven or eight inches each.

I'd saved a huge ledge pool for the evening and much hoped no one had taken it. The pool can fish two people comfortably: one at the head, and in the few hundred yards of channel that lead into it, the other at the tail of the pool, where you could position yourself to fish the point of the current just off the end of the rock, a far eddy or two, and the tail itself, where good fish often foraged in the evenings.

I recommended the tail to Knox, and he tried it for a half-hour without raising a fish and then got out and went up to the head. "Beautiful water," he said. "I'd love to see a fish rise, though."

Me, too. I sat on a rock and fussed a bit with my flies and leaders, using my special magnifying attachment to my glasses. As my eyes grow weaker, I find myself taking more and more time *before* I fish, to make sure all is in order; it's becoming harder to do so *on* the water.

A fish rose, then another.

They were the slow, heavy rises of good fish.

Knox tried immediately for the one near the head of the pool, raised it, followed it upstream, and I didn't see him for more than an hour. I got in at the bottom of the pool, worked my way slowly into position, and promptly raised and caught the fish I'd seen rise.

Then, as if rising to the upsweep of a baton, the pool exploded. I'm the worst of entomologists, but an idiot could have seen the dozens of huge mayflies that could only have been Green Drakes, the smallish Blue-Winged Olives, the two or three brands of caddis. There were so many rises you'd have thought it was raining. "Ah, sweet mystery of life!" I hummed, marshaled all my discipline, and began to pick off the trout one by one, starting with the nearest. There was so much fly on the water you could have caught fish on anything except a rabbit's foot. And these were large browns, up to sixteen and seventeen inches.

I used only one Gray Fox Variant, never broke it off or had to change leaders, did not fall in, did not hook myself in the ear, and must have taken and released ten or twelve fish when I saw Knox come back around the bend.

I had called him, wanting him to take my spot, and had almost waded upstream: but the moment was too hypnotic; I could not move.

Had he caught anything? I'd feel terrible if he hadn't, but there were still forty-five minutes of fishing left and fish were still rising steadily in some interesting lies.

"How'd you do?" I called.

"Want to go?" he said. "We've got a long trip back."

So I'd caught a halcyon night, *finally*, and a good friend had been locked out. "Try down here," I said. "They're still rising."

"I've had enough."

I reeled in and waded out. We turned once to look at the pool, still pocked with fish rising, and headed through the woods toward the hayfield where we'd parked our car.

"Did you get some fish, old friend?" I asked.

"Yes, I got some fish." His voice was deadpan, steely.

"Many?"

"Yes," he said, "many."

"That's terrific. I'm thrilled," I said.

"It was only one of the best night's fishing of my life," he said.

It was nearly dark now and he could not have seen me smile. I steeled my nerves against some dull but honest prose and said: "It was one of the best night's fishing of my life, too—and it's good to think you get one like this now and then."

BAD POOL

"A foolish consistency is the hobgoblin of little minds," says Emerson. "With consistency a great soul has simply nothing to do." Not being one of the big fly-fishing souls, I have often lingered with an old, outmoded idea long after the rest of the fly-fishing world has given it up as archaic.

Some of this is pure sentimentality. We love what we know well and we often love the "spirit" of something more than its performance. Take bamboo. It has soul. It has character. It comes from a single man's passion and skill. I can never use a fly rod by the late Dennis Bailey without remembering what he once told me about his decision to become a rodmaker. He had killed a man. It was an accident, on the road, and the court did not finally hold him responsible; but the event shocked and shook him and made him quit a lucrative job in industry and seek to do something with his life that would bring beauty and pleasure into this world. He began to make bamboo rods. In Coventry, England, he began to make them with immense care and imagination, developing designs devised by Charles Ritz, experimenting with a unique oak handle, adding a special screw-locking reel seat, using the old-style intermediate windings that require such undying patience. The rod he gave me, signing it to me on the butt, is gorgeous.

Intermediate windings may not be the most practical feature on a fly rod: in fact, they are not necessary any longer and even add a bit of weight. But done by a master, they also add a touch of old, nearly forgotten elegance to a tool now made of awesomely practical space-age materials. I am not too busy or too practical a fellow not to want a bit of old elegance in my life now and then.

And I often think of the wise old judge Robert Traver, and his exclusive love of bright, wild brookies in nearby water that he knows and loves. Not for him excursions to far-flung corners of the world for one-week stands. Not for him the itch of newness. He likes the simple quality of what he knows well and has lived with—consistently. He likes the solitude and the texture, the expectation of returning to his familiar "Frenchman's," the gentle variations, the constants, the tin cup and the bourbon, morels in the woods, intriguing rock formations back among the trees, the smell of Upper Michigan cedar, days that brush the heart with their intimacy.

Sentimental? Perhaps. But a life mostly filled with sentiment, feeling, rather than mere exploit.

When a friend showed me a pool (call it the Big Bend) eight years ago, and that first day we caught a pip of a Hendrickson hatch and outsized wild browns feeding freely, I fell in love at first sight. I decided I had finally found a spot worthy of my most patient consistency.

What a glorious pool it is. The water sweeps down from a four-hundred-yard-long riffle, hits the bend, and makes marvelously trouty music. There is a huge rock, the size of a Buick, in the middle, and a long twisting eddy below. I've found strong rainbows in the near run and gigantic browns in the main eddy. The pool itself must drop to fifteen or eighteen feet, and when the sun is right and the water low, you can see the gigantic shadows circling slowly, slowly, near the bottom. "Alligators," a friend calls them.

I raised one of them once, on a huge spider, on the last day of the season, and saw another rise to a twelve-inch chub I'd released—and take it like I munch a sardine.

I dreamed of that day all winter and dreamed too of the times I took four during a Hendrickson hatch and two in June on stone flies. Each year I went back to the Big Bend with my great expectations.

What matter that, the fourth year after I found it, I caught no fish whatsoever in the Big Bend. None rose during a massive Hendrickson hatch; I could not move one in the long glide below the bend, nor in the big flat pool below the glide, nor in the riffles below the pool. I could not think that the pool was fished out. It was too far from the road, too long a trek in for many people to have found it; and it was too maverick, too hard, for anyone but a maniac to love. Even my friend had given it up as a lost cause— rather too summarily, I thought. It remained my reasonably secret pool—but it produced no fish.

I can't say that this much troubled me. I've had quite enough fishless days to know that this is not why I fish. And bit by bit, I began to know the pool more intimately. I discovered that rainbows would rise violently to stone flies in the upper riffles after dark on a late-June night. I concluded that the big flat pool, despite its troutiness, contained only a few smallmouth bass and suckers. The lower runs could be productive in June, with #6 golden stone-fly nymphs, fished deep. I heard there was a good March brown hatch and had that to look forward to. Was there a *Tricorythodes* hatch on July mornings? Would grasshoppers produce in August? Streamers in September? The Big Bend itself, caught at just the right hour, might at any time disclose another of its astonishing mysteries. I had a lifetime to fish *my* Big Bend, the Big Bend of my dreams, and the sure belief that it was worth my best dreams.

So I continued to lean toward the pool when I had the time or when I was heading in that direction. You did not have to expect a pool to produce regularly. It remained interesting. You never knew when you'd hit a day like that first one, or that last day of the season. There were alligators in the Big Bend.

The years passed. There was a flood, then a drought, then a trip to Montana, then a year I could not get to it once, then four, five, six trips when—against the best advice—I chose to fish the Big Bend rather than another part of the river, or another nearby river, and caught nothing. I knew it and I loved it. That was enough. And I had my great expectations.

Last spring, as I waited for reports to begin trickling in from upstate, I kept thinking of making my first excursion to the Big Bend. It haunted my dreams. Fugitive images of the water slipped in and out of my mind. I remembered the particular way the Bend pool was dead all one morning, and how the first dun Hendricksons appeared in the air and the first little splash-rises began. The fish did not stack up in the flats waiting for the flies, as I'd seen them do on other rivers. The mayflies swept down past the rock and the fish hurtled up from the depths of the pool to snatch them. It was exciting, abrupt. The fish took your fly sharply, on the run, with a spurt that sent little shock waves through your chest.

Then the reports had flies coming good on one of the tributary rivers that got its hatches exactly ten days earlier, and I counted the days until I could wait no longer, then stole a day and made the long drive up by myself.

The pool was as I remembered it, and my heart was young and expectant. When a drizzle began, I was even surer that I would make a day of it: the weather was ideal for Hendricksons. But one o'clock came, then two, and I counted exactly three flies and a little cloud of caddis. And then it was three o'clock and the chill set in and no trout had risen and I had moved none, even with nymphs, and I began to think of all the other rivers I could—and should—be on instead.

I happened to *need* a good day. You know: sometimes you go out for pure pleasure and sometimes you go out to exorcise a few demons also. I had a lot of demons in my brain and I needed a truly good day to wash them away. I had come with a winter's worth of dreams and expectations and I was fishing well and the conditions seemed ideal—but the river trampled on the white linen of my dreams with muddy feet.

Eventually, of course, I slipped, fell, and hit my eye on a rock; the large pockets of my Cambrian fly-fisher's coat filled with water and nearly wrenched my shoulders out of joint; when I emptied them, I dropped my Wheatley fly box into the water, half the compartments opened, and I lost most of my flies. Well, I'd been there before. That didn't much matter.

But the charm was broken.

It was time to move on.

You did not have to be a great fly-fishing soul to know that; not even a very small and sentimental sort of soul would miss that message. The hex was on the Big Bend, and I knew that, from now on, despite my most avid longings, I could only call it Bad Pool and seek elsewhere a place worthy of my foolish consistency.

A TALE OF TWO PONDS

"How big did you say the browns run?" I asked.

"Oh, they go to eighteen, nineteen inches—even larger," said Larry. "They've gotten a bit *too* large and lunch on the five-and six-inch stocked fish they put in every fall. It's a real problem."

That was surely the kind of problem I could contend with, so I walked promptly to the dock, and sure enough, this was one of those dark but spring-water-clear ponds, with a muted blanket of umber leaves on the bottom, thirty feet down—a pure New England trout pond—and I knew I was hooked on it.

"Of course we *could* fish it tonight," said Larry, "but I'd rather show you the other lake and get us a mess of pickerel and bass."

Pickerel and bass? I did not for a moment consider what he'd said seriously. Who would?

The ponds are private so I won't tell you their names, which don't matter anyway. Larry belongs to a group in southern New England that owns both of them; he said everyone fishes the trout pond, but only he and one or two other members fish both. When he invited me up and told me about them, and then when I saw the trout pond, I had no hesitation about which I preferred. I discouraged all consideration of the bass and pickerel pond; I dreaded the thought that I might waste some of the weekend on it.

So that first night several years ago we paddled halfway out and began to chase down a few clusters of quietly dimpling rises. Of course these were the evil sort of trout that rise six or seven inches beyond your best cast. Since Larry can cast a flyline a half-mile, that left me out completely—but half on the troll, as dusk turned to night, I felt one good trout take, felt it twist twice, then felt it slip free.

In the morning no fish rose, nor did they during the day.

I began to doubt there *were* trout in the pond. I began to think, sheepishly, of the warm-water pond. In the late afternoon, Larry said he'd show me a couple of trout and then we could do some *real* fishing, so we trolled some plump plugs down near the bottom and hauled up a couple of the prettiest brown trout you could imagine, in the eighteen- to nineteen-inch class. They were gorgeous fish and I'd have loved to take them on a fly; on the troll I hardly felt them do more than wriggle a few times.

"Maybe we'll do better with the bluegills," Larry said as we drove a mile or so down dirt roads to the warm-water pond.

"Larry" is Larry Madison—and he's one of the ablest fly

fishermen in the world; I was amused at his interest in this pond we were headed for, to which he'd been angling me for the past couple of days.

When we got there, and I stood on the weathered dock, I saw at once that it was a fishy lake, a lake with a character that I happened to know well. Where the trout pond was featureless and you had to find the fish either on the bottom or where they rose, this pond had texture and... well, fishiness. It was the kind of water I'd fished when I was a kid, for pickerel, shiners, bluegill, and perch. It had a long shoreline to the left, filled with patches of lily pads, fallen trees, a dozen kinds of rock formations. To the right were half-submerged shrubs and beds of eelgrass and coves. You looked to the shores of such a lake; that's where you wanted to fish with a fly rod; and the shores had dozens of perfectly fetching features.

I remembered South Lake near Haines Falls where I'd first fished for anything, when I was six or five or even younger, and Ellis Pond where I'd fished in my teens, and I thought about vacations with my family on Greenwood Lake and Pontoosuc Lake in the Berkshires, and I remembered the twitch of a bobber and the stab of a pickerel slashing at a hooked shiner and smallmouth bass smashing a Flatfish and the summer on Ellis Pond when I first tried a fly rod and caught bluegills on a bright wet fly twitched back just beneath the surface.

I could make a late afternoon and evening of such a pond without a moment's hesitation: it was almost noxious with nostalgia.

We went to work at once, alternating at the oars, casting in against the textured shoreline. I stayed with the fly rod. I used a little streamer and caught a mess of perch and some bluegills; Larry used a spin-casting outfit and caught perch on practically every cast. In an hour we came to a huge cove laced with lily pads, with patches of open water scattered throughout the field of green and white. The place was lousy with pickerel. I'd cast, then retrieve quite as fast as I could manage, and they'd dart electrically after the streamer. They'd flash at the fly, hit it with astonishing speed, pounce just as I was lifting the fly out of the water. I'd never realized how much fun pickerel could be on a fly rod.

At dusk Larry advised me to cut down the length of my leader and make sure it was twenty-pound-test at the butt; he gave me a huge, shaggy, yellow hairbug, with four long strips of hair at the edges, for legs. He cast now with his own #10 rod a couple of times, and I was impressed at how slowly, powerfully, the rod moved, turning over the big bug easily a full seventy feet away.

I tried a couple of times, found the bug too heavy for the #7 rod, cut back on the leader, and managed to add a few more feet to my casts. The entire feel of the cast was different from fly fishing a small dry fly for trout. But the slower rhythm was hypnotic, and in a short time I was dropping the bug within a foot or so of where it ought to have gone, and I had one swirl, and then a follow that might have been a bluegill with big eyes, and then, just at dark, I was granted a revelation.

It was the kind of revelation that changes lives, or converts, or at least shatters your complacency.

A truly gigantic bigmouth smashed the bug just after I'd twitched it off a lily pad: the bass crashed up, with a rise the size of a bathtub, wrecking the flat surface, wrecking my nerves, rolling twice to flaunt its fat girth, seven or eight pounds of it, and then it slipped the hook.

Back at the dock, while I still shook a little, Larry told me that the very best times to fish for the biggest bigmouths in this lake were on the hottest nights in August: sweltering nights, when you were still sweating at midnight, your clothes stuck to your skin in a dozen places, the lake steamy with mists and flat as a tabletop. You moved noiselessly down the shoreline, he said, barely touching the oars to the surface, casting a big bug into the lily pads, to the edges of the shore. The fish, when they struck, would crack open the surface like a grenade had gone off—and the fish were gigantic. One night he'd come off the water at two or three in the morning and had taken six or seven fish over five pounds and several only slightly smaller.

"Enough to make a man swear off trout forever," he said with a light smile.

"Not quite," I said quickly—not in ponds, where, several years later, Larry and I caught the tip of a *Hexagenia* hatch and made a night of it, nor in streams, to which I have permanently lost my heart.

But then, considering the matter carefully as we laid the rods and boxes in the car, I added: "When did you say we'd fish here again?"

HOME WATER

"At a certain season of our life," says Henry Thoreau, "we are accustomed to consider every spot as the possible site of a house." We want roots. We want an end to the gray, grinding transitoriness of our lives. By extension, at a certain season every fly fisherman considers what might best become his "home water."

It could be a private pond, a half-mile or ten miles of private trout water, a cove in a lake, a section of a shoreline, a couple of bends of a public river that everyone else and his brother consider their home water, too. But something in us hungers for the familiar, the known, the pleasure of fishing water that we know like the freckles on our arms.

There is nothing surprising in this. We can only love what we know well, and "first sight" rarely satisfies. We like the comfortable feeling of fishing up a stretch of water we've fished thirty times before; there was a good brown behind that boulder, another in the riffle near those rhododendrons. A Haystack worked well there in early June, the Gray Fox Variant after that, and a Whitlock Hopper all summer. The fallen tree seems farther downstream this year, perhaps because of the March flood; perhaps that orange flash, near the deeply undercut bank, that hint of a truly big brown trout, will reveal itself more fully this year. Home water is intimate water. There is that about it which you know and no one else knows in quite the same way; there is that about it which infects your dreams, like wine in water, touching every part.

Take such memories and multiply them five, ten, twenty times—until the place becomes an extension of your imagination and you're not entirely sure whether or not some of the times you fished it were real or only dreamed. Hemingway, in his story "Now I Lay Me," has a young man stave off fear of death during war by fishing in his dreams a river he knew well as a boy. He would "fish its whole length very carefully" in his mind, "fishing very carefully under all the logs, all the turns of the bank, the deep holes and the clear shallow stretches..." Sometimes he would fish four or five different streams in the night; sometimes, later, he would confuse the actual with the dreamed.

There is a special pleasure in fishing new water, matching the general knowledge we have about a particular kind of water to a new and specific challenge. The pleasure of fishing "old" water, home water, is different: the water has a history with us; we know how to prompt out some of its secrets; it is the same but, this season, boasts slight changes—and these slight variations in what is remembered are the lovelier for their delicate newness. The Green Drake will hatch in the afternoons in early June on such water, and as you fish up the river, the layers of old memories drift back, fueled by recollection, expectation, that new color to the water, the difference in the air, the presence of caddis, too, this time, new fallen logs, and a fish that splash-rises near a boulder you can't remember, the fish's head the size of a dog's.

Often you'll achieve a special level of excellence on such home water. Lefty Kreh once told me that he'd bet on the knowledgeable local fisherman, on his home water, to catch more and larger fish than the acknowledged pro, fishing it for the first few times, any day. And when the "pro" and the "local" are combined, the skill can be awesome. I used to love to watch Art Flick fish up the riffles and pockets of the Schoharie, flicking his Gray Fox Variant into a score of remembered pockets. He was like a vacuum cleaner. He'd take eight, ten fish for every one I or Mike Migel— with whom we often fished—would raise.

I've had half a dozen pools over the years that I thought of as home water, though I fish none of them today. There was one on the East Branch of the Croton that I fished Opening Days for a hundred years when I was a kid; but it got pounded to death by overfishing and its conformation changed radically when the huge tree, which formed holding pockets upstream and down, was washed away. A part of us gets washed away at such times, too. There's another pool, on another East Branch, that I fished with good friends for ten years, after a halcyon day that was never repeated. I kept trying to make that one a home; I kept coming back to it with the most romantic readiness—and it always sent me packing.

Some years ago I felt that I was in that season of my life when I wanted a more permanent brand of home water. I was in no position financially to buy water, and I knew only vaguely about a number of clubs I might join. In the end I became a member of one that I had fished as a guest ten years earlier; it was old, storied water, long in private hands, and the fee wasn't quite stiff enough to sting. Many of the runs and riffles and pools had names like Oak Run and Hemlock Riffle and Frying Pan Pool, and the first spring before the season started, my nerves buzzed with anticipation. I liked the idea of having home water. I liked the idea of getting to know it well, every foot of it. I liked the idea of fishing it early and late, year after year.

Early one morning in late May, I started at six A.M. and fished the whole length of it, hungry to know it all. I started at the downstream wire with the orange "Posted" sign slung in the middle, in sneakers (so I could travel fast), and fished a dry fly to where the uppermost orange sign hung, three miles upriver. I fished the long flat pools and runs beneath the overhanging hemlocks; I lingered at the pools with names that had grown greater through public print and at pockets that had no names. I fished hard and intensely, and since it was early, and during the week, I met no one. I had my home water to myself, just as I'd always dreamed.

What a memorable day that was, filled with discovery: the grayness when I started; the slowly twisting mists; the first fish that came sluggishly in the flat where the current broke; the sight of those cruising browns—making waves—in the Frying Pan Pool, neither of which I raised; the way the river came alive at nine-thirty with a storm of caddis; and then the deliberate hatch of sulphurs at eleven, and how I could only take two fish from ten that were working.

On other days, when I came back, I went to sections I wanted to know better, that had revealed enough of their mystery to make me hunger for more. I remember lovely days: a spinner fall at the Bridge Pool, when a dozen fish were high in the water and sipping with great selectivity; an afternoon when the riffles danced with caddis and every fish there rose to my fly; a morning when the sulphurs came, and then kept coming, and I took nine trout and walked away from a pool still pocked with the rises of feeding fish, smiling like a baboon.

Getting to know the water better, I scored better; discovering some secrets, I pursued others; I loved the water and I shared it with a few close friends, and in the winter I dreamed fifty times of fishing it, from "Posted" sign to "Posted" sign, and those dreams mingled with days I actually spent on the water.

And then I quit the club.

At first I could not tell precisely why. Was it my chronic restlessness? Was it some wild thing in me that wants never to be ritualized or standardized or muzzled? And why would I think the club was doing that to me?

I don't know.

Oh, I know I'll miss it. I know when I've spent a fruitless day banging away at some stretch of unknown water, whose only denizens may be muskrats for all I know, I'll wish I were back there, fishing water I'd grown to love so much. I'll miss it when I find a dozen guys pounding a favorite pool on public water with spinning lures. I know too that I won't miss it when I turn the corner of some new stream and see water and challenges that make me shiver with pleasure, that have me talking to myself.

I don't really know why I quit the club—except that, just possibly, I found home water too comfortable. Or maybe I'd rather be hunting for *new* home water.

THE QUIET PLACE

All that summer, whenever we went to the old club property, I fished the pond. The stream was heavily stocked and held a few truly good fish; in the past, ever since the first week the club had become public water, I had fished the stream with great pleasure.

It was small but spring-water clear; at times the trout could be prima donnas, demanding the choicest flies, expertly presented. But I was tired that year and preferred to take the old wooden rowboat out behind the island and cast up into the channel. The oars creaked loudly in the oarlocks as I rowed; the boat leaked.

It was a quiet place, a still pond riffled only slightly at the head by a lazy current, surrounded by old birch and alder and pine. The club had once been exclusive, with thousands of acres fenced private and wild in the midst of the neon hurly-burly of our time: a place almost antique—protected, preserved, quiet. Of another time and place. It was still fenced and nearly wild, and the pond was the quietest place within the quiet acres. It provided a retreat, and that year I needed rest. I did not want to be challenged.

In July and August, on several rainy afternoons and on several when the sun was hot and bright, I would row away from the battered wooden dock by myself, or perhaps with Henry or Mike or Mari in the boat with me, up the far side of the island and into the pocket pool below the little inlet bridge. I would lower the cast-iron anchor, tie on a nymph or streamer, and make cast after methodical cast up into the head of the current, letting the fly sink, then retrieving it slowly.

It was not exciting fishing and I enjoyed it for precisely that reason. My head was tired; my heart was a dried prune. So I sat in the old wooden rowboat in the middle of this still pond in the middle of the preserve, and all that summer I fished in that slow, methodical way.

The brookies in the pond were fat—up to about two pounds —and occasionally I took an old rainbow of eighteen or nineteen inches, with an outsized head, almost golden sheen, and shrunken body. I could always count on five or six good fish when I fished the pond and one afternoon caught closer to twenty.

As I fished it the third and then the fourth time that summer, I realized I needed the regularity of the pond. It was a generous place, outside the mystery and ambiguity that I usually value so highly. I could depend upon the pond. It was a reliable place, a quiet place. Now and again some wood ducks would shatter the silence; once I saw a wild turkey come close to the shore and watch me with its nervous, bobbing head—and I paused and stopped casting and watched it. I was in no hurry. I knew the fish were there; I knew I would get some; I was after something else, and fishing that pond was its portal.

I came to the pond, as I said, for peace—for the predictability of catching a few good fish. The fishing was routine, unhurried. I sat in the old rowboat, usually alone and in the rain, water dripping down my cheeks, a strange smile on my face, dreaming. The year had been filled with the miasma of death. A close friend, two close kin—people I loved—were no longer here. I had cleared and cleaned two apartments to the last sweep—discovering those odd hidden corners of their lives that made their nightmares mine. I tried to readjust myself to a world without them, to fill the place in my brain where they had been. I kept seeing these people, hearing them talk; dramas we had played out together suddenly replayed themselves in my mind, unfinished yet, unresolved. Some of the dramas went back to days when I was five or six, and some of them, like most things in my life, were intertwined with fishing, inseparable from it. I remembered days when I was very small and ran, escaping, to another pond and fished in another way, with bobber and bait, and those days remained sharply etched in my mind. I cast out, perhaps practicing my new double-haul, and let the fly sink and then retrieved it the same way each time. Caught in the slow rhythm of the thing I could look around me while I fished: at the old wooden bridge, the spot where the current brushed an overhanging branch and kept it in perpetual motion, almost as if it were alive. I could watch the changing formations in the sky, the brush for some new species of bird, one of the tame deer; I often looked down into the opaque waters in which lines angled to the point of a cone and disappeared, like lives.

Not nearly on every cast, perhaps only once in twenty or thirty, the line would tighten, the rod bend down and throb. I would stand, take the line against the butt of my rod with my right index finger, reel in the slack with my left hand, and play in one of those good generous fish.

I went for one last time that year on the last day of the season. It was a raw day, gray and chill, with periods of sharp, cold rain breaking the constant drizzle. The trees were a rosy umber, tinged with yellow. I went with Mike, who usually fished the stream, and we dressed in ludicrous yellow slickers and rainpants, bundled against the cold, and had to bail out the old rowboat with a rusty can before we could step in. There were curled leaves on the water and twigs and dried grasses.

"I can guarantee you four or five good brookies," I said.

"That's what I'm worried about," said Mike. "It's too easy. Maybe I'll try the stream."

"I can use one more easy day," I said. "One more day like the others I had this summer. And your company ain't bad."

Mike rowed, and on my first cast a small brookie charged the yellow flash of my Edson Tiger and hooked itself.

"We'll get a dozen like this," I said, smiling, "only bigger. You'll see."

"That's what I'm afraid of," said Mike.

"None of them are too big. But we'll get a batch of them."

We came around the far side of the island and anchored in the heart of the pool, and I cast out just as I had cast all summer. Twenty, forty, eighty times I cast up against the old wooden bridge, let the fly sink deep down into the channel, and retrieved it slowly. Not a tap. Nor did Mike have one.

"Guaranteed?" he teased.

We thought that perhaps they had moved out of the deep pool, into shallower water, and tried first along the far, then the near, shore. Nothing. We tried under the large branches at the tail of the pond, near the dock, near submerged rocks and along grass shallows. We switched flies and varied our retrieves. They were having none of it.

After several hours the rain came hard and dripped over our faces and we kept chattering away about fish we had once caught or lost, waters we had fished together; we dreamed and laughed together. I did not think that I was not thinking of those other things. I did not think of them at all.

"Too easy?" I asked as it grew gray, then dark, and we rowed back to the old dock.

"It was delightful," said Mike.

In the headlights, while we talked and drew down out rods, an attendant came up and asked whether we had seen or hooked the eight-pound brown that had gotten into the pond.

"*Eight* pounds?"

"Every ounce of it."

"That's a big fish," I said. I looked toward the pond.

"Very big," said Mike.

"But we had a good day. Not too easy," I said.

"It was a joy."

"That eight-pounder would probably have spoiled every-thing," I said, smiling. "Too exciting. Too much action for us."

"Maybe," said Mike.

"Anyway, there are some big rivers, wild rivers, I'm thinking of trying next year."

"You sure they won't be too challenging?" Mike asked.

"Not hardly," I said.

THE OLD MAN

The old man was there when I came out of the woodline and into the clearing, when I turned the last corner. At first I smiled when I saw him casting from a chair perched on one of the wooden ramps. The Connetquot had dozens of these ramps and I do not like them. "That's the life," I thought, "but not for me."

Then I saw that the old man was sitting in a wheelchair and that he held the slack line for his casts in his mouth.

I had walked briskly that bright, hot autumn afternoon—the last day of the season—and sat down for a few moments to rest at one of the bench-tables near the hatchery. From where I sat I could see only the old man's right side and back. He was using a small bamboo rod and cast ably—his loops tight, his forward thrust authoritative—but not very far. I could not see his face, but I could tell by the way he leaned forward and studied the water that he was intent at his work. And he was surely outfitted for the kill, with a long-handled net propped against the chair, an old wicker creel beside that, a full vest, and a khaki hat with a lamb's-wool band crammed with bright flies.

I watched for ten minutes. He would cast across and slightly upstream, follow the fly down with head and rod, then pick up, false cast once, and cast again. He was catching nothing.

I knew this stretch of what had once been the famous old Southside Club and now was run as a state park. The several hundred yards above the hatchery were reserved for the handicapped and aged. He'd earned it on both counts. A neat little sign at the tail end of the run announced these restrictions. Once, several years ago, I came to the stretch from another road, for the first time, failed to see the sign, saw a dozen fish rising, and got an ego as big as the Ritz when I took just about all of them—and had to smile when I learned from where. The few hundred yards of sap-green water contained hundreds of trout. You could see them holding over the lighter sand bottom between the lines of elodea, or they would bust out from the darker patches of waterweed— three, four at a time—to chase a fly. Too many fish. Far too many. They were too hungry, too unselective. They lacked that critical eye without which gulling a fish becomes child's play.

The old man was catching none of them. His casts were true and the pretty little stream is so small here that he could reach across it. Perhaps his fly picked up too much drag; perhaps he used too large a fly; perhaps the water held fewer trout than the day I fished it. It was the last day of the season: maybe the fish had seen enough artificials and would starve before they'd chase another. I don't know. I rather wanted him to catch a trout. I rather wanted to see him play and land one. Then I would get on with my own affairs, those I had come for, the last rites of not an especially productive season.

Lulled by the quiet of the place and the warm afternoon, tired from my rush to get here, I leaned on an arm, watched the old man, and amused myself imagining this feeble old sport as a young man. Had he been a member of this club? Had he once fished the four-mile length of it, each run and pool of it? Did he resent being condemned to this one rather privileged spot, on a ramp? Did the river's new public role disturb him? Did he resent newcomers and plebians such as me and wooden ramps and the death of an old order? He was old enough—in his late seventies at least—to have fished in the twenties and thirties. What fabulous fishing he might have known! He might have known and fished with Hewitt and LaBranche and Jennings. He might have fished

. . . well, anywhere; he might have caught wild trout in rivers that are polluted or madly crowded now, that were ruined before I saw my first fly. Had he been vigorous and adventurous once? Had he pioneered new waters? Had he been truly exceptional at this game, one of those private, unheralded masters at it—a man quite as good as the experts, and I have known a few, but quite uninterested in the public or commercial aspects of the sport? He certainly cast with distinction, though not far and not consistently well. Even his right arm creaked, hitched, failed to follow through. He was a very old man. Twice his fly slapped on the water. Once it hit an overhanging branch and luckily came free. Had he been disappointed, discouraged to the point of despair, when his body betrayed him? Who brought him here? A son perhaps. Maybe an abler, younger friend. Someone he had once fished beside, as an equal. He was dependent now, tethered to those who could and would help, a burden, an inconvenience. Were they condescending? Did they *pity* him? And what *had* happened to his body? A stroke? An accident? How long ago? His left hand appeared to move not at all; I could see that his legs were pinched together, thin under bulky pants, lifeless. Had he thought when all this happened that it was at last over for him—wading swift streams, tying cunning flies, pursuing sport and mystery and independence and perhaps—like me—his soul in moving water? Perhaps. And perhaps not. He might have been paralyzed fifty years ago, or thirty years ago, or after he retired; he might even have started to fly fish after this mangling of his body took place. Fly fishing in this fashion, as he now practiced it, might be the only kind he knew, his salvation. But I did not think so. There was something too intent in his manner, his gestures, too skillful in his cast. The man had once been a superb fly fisherman. And when you have once done something well, quite as finely and purely as you are able, there must be a deep humiliation in being reduced to such a state. Once his eyes might have seen the quick, bright wink of a trout underwater, on the far side of the river. Once he could fish all day, on any man's river, from first light until the hushed gray of dusk. Once he could fit a 7X leader point through the eye of a #20 fly the first time he tried. Once he could tie midges, wrap rods, move lithely in a river, become one with it. Once. Had he slipped slowly over the years, so slowly he could not feel the fine edge vanish? Was this to be his last time out, a final trip, a last fling at it before a winter he might not survive? Had he stopped *liking* to go out—worn down by the cruelty of expectations, the blunders, the memories? How much did he hurt from being unable to do what he had once done with such delight, what he was now reduced to practicing crudely and in the tamest of places?

I could not see his face. I could not tell.

Now and again he leaned perilously forward to get an extra foot or two to his cast. He strained. Then he put his fly firmly into an overhanging branch. He pulled the line taut with his mouth, grasped the line with his rod hand, pointed the rod at the place where it was hooked, and pulled straight back. He could not do it. On his third try I found myself rising from my seat to help him. On his fourth try the leader broke.

Then he retrieved line, brought the leader to his mouth, leaned the rod against the chair, secured a fly box, and out of my sight, fumbled for ten minutes before he was ready to fish again. He appeared now to have some little use of his left hand. Once he raised it—clawed and crabbed—and held the fly to the light. Before he cast, he let the fly hang loose from the propped-up rod, cupped his right hand under his right leg, and raised the leg and repositioned it a few inches to one side.

I went off then, restless as always, brooding, making up fantastic stories, remembering the boy I once was, barefoot in a mountain creek as clear as truth, as cold as snow.

As always, I was glad to be on the water. I piddled here and there and found a few large brookies camped under a long willow branch and coaxed them out; I made some blunders you'd have thought impossible; and after the sun had vanished and the sky was merely bright gray, I returned to clean my few fish on the bench-table near the hatchery.

I had forgotten the old man.

He was there on the ramp. But now his rod was sharply bent. Twenty-five feet downstream a heavy brook trout rolled and pocked the surface. The old man held his rod high and the arc grew sharper. Then the fish turned. Then, in a few minutes, I could see the white of it on the surface, and the man was transferring the rod to his crabbed left hand, supporting it between his legs. For a moment he faltered. I found myself rising to help him. Then he grasped the long-handled net with his right hand, lowered it, and scooped up the fish.

It was a pretty brookie, all right—plump, bright, about seventeen inches.

"Bravo," I said softly. "Well done, old man."

And then he turned, still holding his trout in the net; he turned, looked around him, saw me, held his trout a bit higher, and smiled. I saw his eyes. I looked closely, beyond the crabbed body, at his eyes. His eyes, large and bright behind thick glasses, were smiling, too.

3

OUT WEST

WILD STRAWBERRIES

There is a picture of me taken last summer, holding a trout in one hand, a graphite fly rod in the other. I am standing near a cluster of lodgepole pine, near the brief falls of a meadow creek. It is a color photograph and the river is tawny, speckled with silver. The spots on the fish, a brookie, are bright red. I am quite ridiculously plump.

Dave took the photograph. We had followed the creek from its confluence with a famous trout stream high up into a second and then a third meadow. We had leapfrogged—first one of us fishing a bend or pool while the other watched, then the other fished. We are good old friends and it was a truly bright summer afternoon and we were in no particular hurry. So we fished slowly, and we talked when we felt like it, and we tried to make our few casts count.

Had someone been watching us from the tree line he could have told easily that the silver-haired man was by far the more adept fly fisherman. He would have seen that man show his portly friend how to stand ten or fifteen feet back from the bank and how to cast so that only the leader and fly rolled over the little hedgerow of grass that bordered the creek and fell into the water. Twice he would have seen the silver-haired man kneel, bend low, cast to a pool, wait, cock his head, and then suddenly strike. He might not have heard the splash behind the high tufts of grass, but he would have seen the rod bend in that happy arc and the portly man walk up quickly to be near his friend while each fish was played and released. Both fish were rainbows. They were as silver as the man's hair.

Had someone been watching, he would have seen that the portly man (whose girth was of such a fine, full dimension that it threatened to split his waders if—as he was told to do—he knelt) wasn't catching any. If there was some little trick or mannerism that his friend was employing, he did not see it. He managed to cast quite honorably; from a distance he might even have looked adept. And he quickly picked up the technique of dropping his fly over the grasses. But he caught nothing.

I looked back into the woods, wondering how we looked, but no one was watching us. We had the river very much to ourselves. I liked it that way. We followed the meandering creek from one S-turn to another, one after the other, and fished the deeper bends and a few of the back reaches where the creek narrowed to no more than several feet wide and was perhaps five feet deep. It was leisurely, fascinating fishing. There were sometimes big browns in such water, Dave said—alligators; he had caught them. They came up from the main river to escape the late-summer heat, and you had to tempt them with a large fly into doing what they did not particularly want to do. As I cast, I imagined a ridiculously large splash behind the tuft of grass and the fight of an eight-pound brown in such small water. The fish were there for the coolness of the water, for the respite, not for the regular business of foraging. But they could be caught.

Dave had tied the flies we used. In fact, they were a new version of an old and famous fly he had invented, and they imitated grasshoppers. We were a little early for grasshoppers, though there were a few small ones in the meadow, and perhaps we were a little early for the run of truly large trout out of the main river. Perhaps not. There were a few fish to be caught and Dave was catching most of them. That's a habit of his. The air had a habit, I remembered, of being warm and fresh on days such as this in Montana, and it was. The sky was brilliant blue, with evanescent shreds of clouds. On another day I might have been troubled that I was not catching any fish whatsoever, a habit of mine. This day it was more a source of quiet amusement than displeasure. I enjoyed seeing my friend catch a few good fish and I enjoyed hearing him tell me the fish had come to the fly "like a beggar to a five-dollar bill."

We had fished steadily for about two hours, leapfrogging, before we came to the second meadow. Here there were hot-spring seepages and a tawny tint to the water. All was wilder. The fields were flecked with the white, yellow, crimson, purple of wildflowers. The mud near the seepages bore the tracks of many elk, and we saw several elk back in among the pines. Along some stretches, the creek was no more than a few inches deep and a half-dozen feet across; there was no cover, no protection for a truly large fish here. What they wanted was what I had come up this creek for: a respite.

What a wearing, forgettable, wearying year it had been. How often I had felt like Eliot's "pair of ragged claws scuttling across the floors of silent seas"—quite unbrained, disembodied, and my body blowing up like a blimp. To pay the piper, the bamboo was gone, books would follow: a year without color or taste, without rivers, without words.

I had snatched at a chance to come West, but that first week had been a tumult of conferences. There is a business and a politics to fly fishing, even as there is to everything else. Some of it must be done, and often good people do it and advance the sport and protect such rivers as the one I was fishing, without which there would be no sport. I admired the work and many of the people who did it—but I had an itch to be alone, not in crowds. Now there were a few days and I wanted to see if rivers and woods could work their dark magic again. I had a few good tools left and I wanted simply to fish again.

The little creek was there—splattered with foam and winding its tawny way through curve after curve, down to the main river. It was the smallest of waterways, but it held promise. The big browns might be there. They might bust up behind the grasses and shatter my heart. Now and then I cast into the creek and waited, and then cast again.

In the late afternoon, I sat on some roots covered with lichen and moss, took off my glasses, smoked a pipe slowly, and watched Dave fish. He took several small fish, then stooped and poked into the grasses a moment. I thought he was collecting insects.

"You won't believe how these taste," he said, standing up.

"I'm not sure I'm ready to try."

When he came over to where I sat, I saw he had a handful of small wild strawberries.

A dozen of them were soft and crimson in my hand. You could not press them or they'd squash. I held them gingerly for a moment, then popped them, one at a time, into my mouth.

Dave picked a batch more and I put them all up to my mouth at once, smearing my lips. They were the choicest of foods, astonishingly sweet and tart, an emblem of something.

In a few minutes I stood, walked to the creek, and cast into the bubbles and swirls where the brief falls met in the pool. A fish snapped at the large grasshopper, hooked itself, fluttered at the surface, and I hoisted it in.

As I raised the fish, Dave said, "We really ought to record this trophy," and snapped his camera twice.

In the photograph, which I took out and grinned at a bit too often all year, the man is smiling rather smugly. The brookie—its little crimson spots the color of wild strawberries—is barely four inches long. The man appears to be either a lunatic or a clown. Or perhaps he's merely giddy with the pleasure of having returned to a thing he was born to do, and to write about, for as long as there are rivers and for as long as he has words to write and there are a few people who want to read them.

THE DIRECTOR

There was fear and trembling among the outfitters and guides of West Yellowstone when news reached them that "Fast-Fly" Lyons was scheduled to direct a month's program last summer at a local fly-fishing and conservation foundation. And with good cause.

When ten thousand fly fishermen signed up for Fast-Fly's

clinic, seminar, whatever it was, would any of them ever again need an outfitter or guide? Fast-Fly would surely give away all the best spots within fifty miles, instruct so that instruction would never again be needed, and offer cheap (Fast-Fly is nothing if not cheap) what elsewhere has become so dear.

In fact, Fast-Fly's first week was somewhat undersubscribed. He waited for an hour that first morning but no one appeared. He was a director with no one to direct. How could anyone pass up this magnificent cheap chance? he wondered. Clearly he was the bargain of a lifetime.

Finally, one customer showed up. Well, he did not actually show up. He left a message that he would be the tall, thin guy in the gray sweater in one of the local fly shops, and if Fast-Fly so chose, he could look him up. Fast-Fly did not hesitate to so choose. He ran to the shop in search of a tall, thin, gray sweater.

The lucky fellow's name was Les Ackerman, and he had been fishing the West Yellowstone area every day since early June. It was now late July and a Monday.

A truly wise guide neglects no opportunity to learn, even when he is learning from his customer. (One honest outfitter so represented himself in an advertisement several years ago—as someone who was not too proud to learn from those he guided—and is now apparently out of business, if he ever got any.) But Ackerman sounded as if he knew what of he spoke, and Fast-Fly thought he would give the man the unique opportunity to learn the guide's trade. So several times that week he suffered Acker-man to drive him to interesting new spots on the Madison and the Gallatin, and Fast-Fly watched his mentor-customer catch numer-ous fine and noble trout. Fast-Fly was not in the least troubled to learn that Ackerman, who was skillful with the long rod and knowledgeable about the how and where of local fishing, had begun to fly fish seriously only a year or so earlier. He did not write any articles about fly fishing; and he had read less than a dozen books about the sport; and not least, he lived in Dallas. He merely fished well and caught trout and was of wise counsel to Fast-Fly Lyons, who needed quite as much wise counsel that week as he could catch.

Meanwhile, in every spare moment, Fast-Fly whizzed around

the middle Madison and the Henrys Fork and a dozen other rivers
—for the West Yellowstone area has a great plethora of fine trout
water, more than a man could fish in a lifetime—and he looked
for spots where he might take his clients the next week—a week
that would surely boast many times more clients. Hundreds, perhaps.

In pizza joints and from behind bushes, Fast-Fly listened for
those telltale hints of where the big fish were. There were rumors
that Hebgen Lake was hot and that Henrys was cold. Someone
spoke of the Yellowstone's being high and the Gallatin's being low.
Listening, in the West, can be a dramatic experience, given a
certain high diction now and then. He heard that someone had
lost "Mr. Plump" on the Madison, and someone else had been
"hog haulin'" in the Canyon. Fast-Fly listened with wide eyes as
Fred Arbona whispered half-sentences and hints about certain
"tortugas" to be found in remote ponds—huge brookies, the size
of logs, you couldn't believe the size of them, and when they
nosed up to a little streamer you'd cast in the path of one of them,
you'd nearly die of the tension. So Fast-Fly slept, that night and
for many nights thereafter, while visions of tortugas danced in his
head.

To sharpen his thinking, he floated one mighty river with a
true guide one day, sponging up information he might later use.
But when the Mackenzie River boat docked, a local angler's wife
looked at him and said: "You're from New York. I could tell."
Fast-Fly had not said a word. Now that he was a director, almost a
true guide himself, he had been anxious—like Lawrence of Ara-
bia—to be accepted by the natives and to become a native himself. How had this sensitive lady found out? What had he done
wrong? And then he remembered that, when he took off his
waders, his pants had come off, too, and it was clear that the good
local people merely assumed that everyone from the East exposed
himself.

The second week provided a unique opportunity.
There were no clients.
Not even Les Ackerman—who was signed up for every week
but figured he'd learned enough about guiding, which was the
only opportunity Fast-Fly could give him.

So Fast-Fly explored further. He accepted Dwight Lee's in-vitation to fish one evening up a road called Mosquito Gulch. This might be an absolutely unique place to take his clients the next week, when surely all of them would appear. Dwight had some trouble finding the spot up Mosquito Gulch, but then he finally did and they got out and followed the river for a mile downstream, where they fished steadily for a few hours and Fast-Fly was bitten so often by mosquitoes that he felt he had become a single throbbing lump. Had they caught more than three fish, no more than four inches long apiece, he might have remembered the spot, but on the long drive back to town he did everything he could to forget about the place. He would have thanked Dwight for the interesting new experience, but his lips had been bitten so thoroughly and enthusiastically by the mosquitoes that he could only mumble something about the need to make such a place well known to people to whom you'd like some harm to come.

It was not until the third week that some customers finally appeared, anxious to learn from that dazzling international sport Fast-Fly Lyons.

And despite his worst fears, the week went marvelously well.

The group could not have been made up, he thought, of nicer fellows. There was Russ Willis from Seattle and George Burrows from Michigan; Bill Johnson had come up from Texas, and Donn Griffith, a veterinarian, had driven in from Ohio. And Les Ackerman reappeared. Griffith, who was still learning the fly-fisherman's skills, had a marvelous evening and was con-verted fully to the fly. Russ Willis, who could cast a fly half across the Madison—by virtue of a couple of decades of double-hauling for steelhead—needed only a quiet word or two about fishing the *edges* of the current in the Madison to have several startling evenings. And Johnson and Burrows both took fish, including several on the Henrys Fork on a particularly blistering summer evening. And the group talked about the rivers of the area and the need to protect them, and the essential message of conserving and protecting became an integral part of pursuing and catching.

So by Friday, Fast-Fly was quite pleased with himself and

thought himself considerably abler than he'd thought, and he decided to share with his new friends a spot on the Firehole that he had once—six years earlier—fished with great success. It was one of his favorite spots, and he had been reluctant ever to take even his best friends there.

So they set out, in six cars, and slowly wended their way into Yellowstone Park. He felt it incumbent upon himself to stop and point to an elk in the run above Grasshopper Bank and a series of deep holes about which they had spoken during a slide show the night before, and he felt really quite comfortable in this role of genial guide until he turned off the main highway onto a dead-end road and went about a mile and then realized, with a shock, that he didn't have the foggiest idea where he was.

This was a terrible predicament.

It was a miserably hot August afternoon and he was on a dead-end road and he really had no idea whether his secret spot was or was not within twenty miles of where he stopped.

There was no room for the six cars—patiently waiting one after the other—to turn around. He had no idea what was ahead, other than a dead end. And he was pouring sweat and wondering whether he should just throw up his hands, abandon the car, and run to the tree line and live thereafter with the bear and the moose.

But he got a good grip on himself, walked pleasantly past three cars without saying a word, and stopped next to Bill Johnson's station wagon. This was a stroke of genius. Johnson, a wise old Texan, told him exactly where they were and how to get to the section of the Firehole he wanted to fish, and Fast-Fly swore eternal loyalty to this good man who should have been guiding him.

But when they got to the secret section of the Firehole and tested the water, it was at once clear to Fast-Fly that he had made a small miscalculation. The Firehole did not fish best in August. It was better for bathing in August—or for boiling eggs.

Well, Fast-Fly is safely back in the East now, and the guides and outfitters of West Yellowstone are surely safe from his devastating raids and depredations, and he's fixed his trousers and vowed never to guide again—should someone go perfectly loony and ask him—and he deeply appreciates the nice Christmas card he got from one of his clients, quoting the immortal words of Ann Landers, otherwise not much of an authority on the subject: "If you want to catch a trout, don't fish in a herring barrel."

WHERE TO GO

I was in Vernal, off U.S. 40 in northeastern Utah, pursuing with my friend Thom Green rumors of gargantuan bluegill—which, from where I come, is a long way to go for bluegill—when Thom told me: "You realize, Nick, that you have an obligation to your readers to tell them exactly where you've been."

I was not so sure.

"Let them find their own bonanzas," I said.

"That's the wrong attitude. That's what they're buying the magazine to have you do for them. That's what you're paid to do."

"Not that I've found so very many hot spots," I said reflectively.

"Still, when you do . . ."

"But do you know what happens when someone announces such a place in a magazine with one hundred thousand or two million readers? Such publicity can wreck a river or a lake overnight. Someone goes there a year later and they think you've lied; but you've really *caused* the disaster. There are places, Thom, where you can get trampled to death during a Green Drake hatch because someone has been just a little too explicit about his where-to-go."

Thom knew that. He had seen it happen. But he insisted I had an obligation.

"The first thing," I said, "you get none of the solitude that brought you there. Everyone and his mother-in-law are suddenly flogging the river to its doom. Then the size of the fish goes down. One year the average size is five pounds, the next it's three, and then you're fishing for guppies. If someone's subscription is a month late, they're liable to find something that looks like a New York street after a blackout." I was becoming hysterical; nothing looks quite that bad.

"Still," Thom said, "that's what you've been paid to do; that's what readers want. They get two weeks' vacation and they want reliable information, not mystery lakes. You shouldn't take an assignment if you don't expect to produce hard facts."

"But does everyone want to vacation where everyone else is vacationing? If you tell everyone about a posh lodge in Canada that costs three thousand dollars a week, you won't get many takers, not with taxes what they are, but if you mention a public river, you'll spoil it. No. I'd rather go into the worm business than become a popularizer of secret spots. Some writers even make a profession of such discoveries, to the loss, Thom, of their immortal souls. I saw one writer photographed on *four* different rivers— all of which are now on the decline—with the same eight-pound brown trout!"

Thinking of photographs of big fish, we could not help noting, as we walked in and out of several Vernal tackle shops, that all had dozens of unique shots pasted on the walls near the cash register. They were Polaroids mostly, with one unusual feature in common: they were of positively gigantic trout. Eight-, nine-, and ten-pound fish. We had not come for trout, but these were irresistible. Were they from Flaming Gorge? Perhaps we could catch some on a fly designed to imitate the reservoir's principal trout food: Rapala lures. No. They were from Jones Hole Creek.

Anyway, we were in a regional storm and the lake we had intended to fish was unfishable. Perhaps we could amble over and snoop around this new discovery.

Jones Hole Creek. What a lovely mysterious name. And true. You can find the place on any local map. And those big trout, dozens of them, had all come from Jones Hole Creek within the past two weeks. No question about it. Here was an unexpected story: "Lyons Clobbers Trout in Unknown Bonanza." I had written some stories on which bored Madison Avenue editors, in a fine frenzy, had slapped such a title—but I had never found more than two cents' worth of a bonanza in my life.

Nor was there any mystery about the place. Not only would the tackle dealers readily tell of the creek, but the Vernal Chamber of Commerce had a printed map of how to get there, which looked simple enough. How to get there. Ah, dear. Not only "where" but "how." The ultimate sin. Well, this time I would see and catch and tell. The townspeople, photographed in flagrant numbers and in flagrant pride with their monster trout, did not seem shy or secretive. If they did not care, why should I? Let Jones Hole Creek be damned.

So we started out, Thom and I and also W. Earl West, Jr., and Dr. Ed Reasoner from Casper, Wyoming, in Ed's van—and I swore to them all that I would tell everything this time, the whole truth.

It was only a forty-mile drive, mostly over paved road (except, the brochure mentioned, from mileage 16 to 25.5). For my readers I want to be very explicit about how to get to Jones Hole Creek. At mileage 2.9 there is a junction, at which you take the left road. You take the left road again at 7.8 and then the right road, across Brush Creek, at 10.0. At 15.7 there is another junction and you must keep left; the right road is a dead end. The sagebrush begins to give way to cedar and piñon pine here, the brochure says, but frankly I did not notice: we were climbing slowly upward now, hitting the unpaved section (which I did notice), and executing a series of sharp horseshoe turns on a dirt road with no railings. Actually the road is not dirt after a rain. It had rained quite heavily that particular morning. We squooshed our way up the sloshy, muddy ruts, looking down into an eight-thousand-foot drop. My stomach felt approximately that deep.

"Put the car into low gear," said Earl.

"Mind your own business," said Ed.

I was not particularly in the mood for bad Casper, Wyoming, jokes and elected at 21.2 miles not to look out the window anymore, not even when Earl pointed to Diamond Mountain and told the story of how two 1870s hustlers named Arnold and Slack salted it with diamonds and got a San Francisco syndicate to raise ten million dollars; those investors must have been as light-headed as I now was. At least not many people could travel a road like this: Jones Hole Creek was surely loaded with lunkers. Those in the pictures were the size of baseball bats.

After having not spoken for fifteen minutes, nor done anything but pray quietly, I launched compulsively into a story I once heard about a man who came back to an eastern hotel with several outsized brook trout. When asked where he got them, he gave detailed instructions ending with the general caution: "One small problem, though. Rattlesnakes. Once you get past the fallen oak and the quicksand, if the mosquitoes—they're the size of hummingbirds—don't get you, the rattlesnakes will. They lie on the rocks, dozens of them. I've seen them hanging from the trees. But those brookies! You really ought to try Rattlesnake Creek."

I finished the story and Thom said, No. Jones Hole Creek could not possibly have rattlers. The Chamber of Commerce recommended the trip for little kiddies, along with Dinosaurland. It had to be safe.

At 22.3 we passed Diamond Gulch Junction on the plateau. At 25.5, hallelujah, we reached paved road again; but at 31.0 we began a severe descent into the narrow and rugged canyon that I was quite sure would be my final sight. It was not. At 40.0 we finally reached the Jones Hole National Fish Hatchery that stood at the head of the creek. The forty miles had taken nearly two hours. I was limp. Had I traveled all this distance to fish in a hatchery?

Now the sun suddenly made a bright appearance; the wind stopped. We saw dozens of birds working in the pit of the canyon. Not only had we found a bonanza, but we were surely there at precisely the right time—there was a gigantic hatch in progress—and not one car in sight!

Unfortunately, a few people had found Jones Hole Creek before us, which was where they fished, not in the hatchery. An old Fish & Game hand with a narrow, bumpy face and the scratchy voice of truth said: "Well, there was some big fish in the crik. Mighty big fish. They come up from the Green for a couple weeks in the early spring. But there ain't none anymore. No, sir. You bet."

"Have they gone back down?" I asked.

"Didn't have no chance to," he said. "We had three hundred people a day up here for two weeks. They got about every one of them trout, you bet. There ain't none anymore. All fished out. Not a one left. No, sir. All gone."

We spent an hour verifying his story. Jones Hole Creek

proved to be a spritely little brook, spring fed, clear as fresh tap water, filled with watercress and rich in streamlife. Mayflies and caddis were hatching profusely. But the old guy was danged right. You bet.

A couple of days later we pursued a rumor that Ray Lake in Wyoming was yielding ten-pound brown trout. The lake had been closed by the Indians of the Wind River Reservation for four years and it sounded like a sure bonanza. But we discovered, five hundred miles later, that it was infested with carp. Thom got a couple on flies, big ones, three- or four-pounders, and they were rolling and jumping out there as if it was a hustlers convention.

I could tell you exactly how to get there from Jones Hole Creek.

But that might be more than you want to know.

TORTUGA POND

You cannot really convince someone who is a lunatic about rivers to give up his passion and turn to lakes and ponds. He'll laugh lightly or smirk or perhaps say, with quiet disdain or superiority, "You don't mean it, do you?" Or simply: "Thanks, but I prefer *moving* water, actually." And if pressed, he'll cite boredom as his main gripe: the boredom of boats and shorelines, the boredom of unvaried, inexplicable water, the boredom, ultimately, of a placid fly on (or under) placid water.

Argument rarely persuades in matters like this. But affection and feeling and experience sometimes do. You try some new brand of fly fishing, and if you try it on the right day, with the right companion, and certain things happen, a connection is made.

Many years ago, dazed by the water-riches of the West, I stumbled upon Henrys Lake in Idaho and it hooked me. I liked the long, rhythmic casts, the slow and studied retrieve, the sudden stop and heaviness and pulsing at the end of the line. All the fishing was below the surface, but I liked it all better when I began to understand about the midmorning damselfly hatches in the shallows and the leeches at night, when I understood a bit more about channels and springs and which insects were found in the pea-green water. I liked the sense of this fishing being new and challenging to me in new ways. I liked the heavier rod and line—its tug at my arms and shoulders—and the sure knowledge that, deep in that lake, on any cast, at any time during the retrieve, I might find myself latched onto a real old goat of a trout, the largest I'd ever hooked.

It happened.

Several times.

I hooked a couple of fish in the famous Glory Hole, before daybreak, that simply moved off steadily, would not be turned, and somehow broke off. Then, at midday once, I was fishing a simple Wooly Worm, with a red tail and grizzly hackle tied over yellow chenille, and a truly gigantic trout took in water shallow enough for me to see the take and turn. I've been known to lie, but I'll steel myself this time and admit that I'd be lying only if I called this thing less than twelve or thirteen pounds; it might have been more. I was fishing between the Glory Hole and Staley Springs, about where Clarence Wright later took an eighteen-pound hybrid.

The lily pads were thick here and the fish managed to twist the line quickly around one, then another, despite some heavy horsing. There was really little to be done. I took an oar out of the oarlock and paddled to the first patch of pads. Then I leaned far down and pulled them up, so I could slip off the two or three turns of line. Then I followed the flyline off to the left, did the same thing, and looked toward the deeper water. The gigantic hybrid, silvery green, was finning easily, not a trifle scared, still tethered to the leader, which was wound a couple of times around the lower end of still more weed. I could see the situation was impossible. The fish was too deep for me to approach with the long boat net, the tangles too complicated to be jostled free by an oar touching merely the tops of the weeds. I waited and thought and then tried the oar . . . and then the gigantic fish wriggled twice and broke off, and I breathed heavily and stopped fishing for the day.

The lure of such outsized, wildly memorable fish kept me

coming back to that lake year after year, though eventually I sought waters where I could fish the surface.

There are other lakes—East and West—and increasingly I have been trying them, too: one on Long Island, several in upper New York State, one in Maine, another in Wyoming. A couple of years ago I tried a float tube for the first time—in Hebgen Lake and Island Park Reservoir—with my friend Lester Ackerman. Tubing had looked like an ungainly, uncomfortable sort of game, but when I got out there and Les showed me how to do it and I'd tooled around a bit, my eyes only a couple of feet from the surface of the lake (which was a wonderland of fly life), and stalked a couple of gulpers, I knew I could stand a bit more of that, too. Gliding backward, I watched the far hillside, ribboned with jack-leg fences, studded with stands of Engelmann spruce. We watched a golden eagle circle the lake and a flock of mergansers prowl the swamp area. I caught a couple of little gray mayflies, imitated them with a #20 Adams Parachute, and began to make some sense of the process. You kept looking for motion—a tail, a swirl, a wake, a rise, a flash of color under the surface, a hatching fly. When you saw movement, the hunt was on.

Despite what the hardcore river man says, all lakes are different. Each requires its own plan of attack. What keeps the serious fly fisherman from them at times is the thought that lake fishing is a chuck-and-chance-it proposition—which it is not. The British lakes have as defined an entomology as most rivers, and if one applies the pleasure and discipline of studying entomology to the fishing of lakes, the rewards can be great. Most British lakes are shallow and filled with insects, though, and a lot of ours, especially the wonderful reservoir systems in the East, are not. Some of ours are deep and dark and mysterious, and few people have found decent ways to fish them with flies. The Pepacton and the Ashokan hold gigantic browns and rainbows but virtually all of the big fish are caught by live-bait fishermen using big baitfish like the sawbelly. There may be a time when the fish are vulnerable to flies fished on or even near the surface but I haven't found it yet.

Craig Mathews once took me to a shallow hidden pond he'd found in the West Yellowstone area. Somebody was walking around town that week calling big fish he'd caught or seen "tortugas," so Craig called his pond Tortuga Pond. It was a long trek in, through mucky terrain, and the place was guarded by battalions of mosquitoes and buffalo flies that seemed the size of bats. But when I saw the pellucid, pale-green water, filled with delicate weed, with the wakes of tortugas everywhere, I was willing to abandon my cheeks and hands to the mosquito and the buffalo fly forever.

There were defined hatches in water like this, Craig said—a damselfly hatch, midges, three or four caddis, a couple of mayflies, and the fish could be as picky as spring-creek browns. With water this clear, casts had to be long and delicate, leaders whisper-thin.

I guess the pond was a hundred feet across and perhaps six or seven hundred feet long. You had to tread lightly and bend low as you walked the one long fishable side, scanning the water for rising or cruising fish. If the cast was not just right, the fish would go by it without a look; if it was right but the fly wrong, there would be a hesitation, a look, and then a slow retreat of a sneer. The fish moved slowly, with care and great deliberation; several times I spooked working fish with merely an extra false cast or two.

Craig got one large fat brown and I pricked one, and then we cast for several hours to fish that loved to thumb their noses even at the accomplished likes of Craig. Each refusal piqued my interest in Tortuga Pond more.

I remember one huge brown in particular, working over a light-sand bottom, so you could see the fish and its shadow, and the opening and closing of its white mouth. I decided to tuck in and fish for it all the rest of the evening if need be, and I tried for it during the last hour of light, while the mosquitoes bit me so ferociously on top of other bites that I thought my face must look like a leper's. I'd cast, let the wind take the fly near the fish, and then retrieve when the fly had passed the shadow. Sometimes the fish grew skittery and moved away, and I'd wait until it came back and settled into its rhythms again.

Bored? Not for a minute. I stalked that fish with intense excitement, occasionally looking off into the distance, where the sun had dropped below the line of the lodgepole pines and I could see two ospreys, in profile on one of the leafless branches, silhouetted against the gray sky.

Toward dsk, when I could barely see that long black shadow beneath the surface, when I had to cant my head and squint to see the fly on the surface, the fish suddenly rose when I was not ready and promptly snapped me off.

I could grow inordinately fond of such ponds.

HEAVEN OR HELL

In the famous story by G.E.M. Skues, a certain Mr. Theodore Castwell, having hunted "to their doom innumerable salmon, trout, and grayling in many quarters of the globe, died and was taken to his own place." As it turned out, this "place" was a splendidly perfect chalkstream, crammed to the gills with truly lovely trout.

Castwell catches one, of about two and a half pounds, on his first cast, and remarks: "Heavens. This is something like."

Then he catches a few more, on as many more casts.

"Heavens," he says. "Was there ever anything like it?"

"No, sir," says his keeper.

But about sixty fish later—all curiously the same size—Mr. Castwell is less sanguine about the river of our dreams. It ain't fun no more. He wants to stop. That's not permitted. Not even at night? No night there. Does he *have* to go on catching those "damned two-and-a-half pounders at this corner forever and ever?" Yup.

"Hell!" he says.

"Yes," says his keeper.

When the story did not terrify me, it amused me no end. It was Dante's Paolo and Francesca—doomed to make love forever and ever: the sweet becoming bitter, more bitter for once having been so sweet. Never ending.

Now there is clearly no such river in this world. Of that I'm quite sure. So there is no need, in this world, to worry. The finest of them—in the very good Reverend Dan Abrams's words—are

"God's holy brew" and put here to pleasure not plague us.

Still, there are rivers and there are days or portions of days on rivers that can prepare us for that day when we're taken to our "own place," wherever that might be, good or bad. Mr. Skues clearly thought that fly fishing, to the exclusion of all else, would send one to the *bad* place, and that too much of a good thing *is* hell.

To further confuse our thinking on this momentous issue, Huck Finn—no Madison Avenue straw man—*wanted* to go to "the bad place." If his nemesis, Miss Watson, a "tolerable slim old maid with glasses on," who drilled him in manners and tried to "sivilize" him, and kept urging him not to scrunch down in his chair, wanted to go to "the good place," he rather thought he'd try for the other.

Like most of us, I always thought I was brave enough to try a dose of Mr. Castwell's hell—or at least some fleeting image of it here, in this place, which is sometimes good and sometimes not so good. Hell, most of us would love to catch a few hours' worth of those "damned two-and-a-half pounders," and there are even some philandering anglers who wouldn't mind playing Paolo or Francesca for a couple of days.

My friend Sandy Bing invited me to fish a river in the West last summer that he had been touting to me on and off for twenty-five years. The ranch owner through whose land the river flowed had granted him the right to bring one guest *once* during the summer.

And I was sworn to forgetfulness.

Dumber guys than me would have suspected something.

Was one day all one needed?

"If Blue Rock Creek is on," Sandy said, "three hours will be enough."

I did not feel that I had earned such a choice experience. I had earlier had a month's dose of the West and it had been most satisfying. There was a profusion of good water where I was staying—from meadow creeks to burly water—and I had tried a dozen different rivers that month. All had provided that special tonic that is unique to the Rocky Mountain states: a mixture of exquisite landscape, fecund waters, and the real possibility, always, of big fish. I had taken eleven browns and rainbows one afternoon, from twelve to nineteen inches, from the catch-and-release section of a river old-timers were saying had returned to nearly forgotten glory. And I found a fish glutting in the riffle a feeder creek made as it drove into a meadow river, fished for it all afternoon, put it down four times, got it to turn once, and then, near dusk, nailed it. It was a rainbow, plump as a football, stuffed to the gills with crickets, hoppers, three species of nymphs, several flying ants, two moths, four caddis flies, a mayfly, and a stone-fly adult. A hungry beggar. A glutton—but somehow selective as hell.

So I didn't really *need* an afternoon on Blue Rock Creek, but I was curious. The subtitle of Emanuel Swedenborg's book *Heaven and Hell* is "from things seen and heard." He wrote about them in astonishing detail. Less a visionary, I have to experience a thing to know it.

Sandy and I met at noon and got to the meadow through which Blue Rock Creek flows about an hour later. At first I could not see the river. I saw only the meadow—and an enormous number of grasshoppers, of every which size and color.

Only when I came up close could I see Blue Rock Creek—otherwise a phantom—and I lost my heart to it at once. It had been fashioned from my dreams. Where we started it was only thirty-five feet across, mountain-brook clear, a few feet deep. We could see no fish and no fish rose. Sandy said they'd be where you'd expect them: along the far shore, near current lanes, behind rocks and logs.

And they were.

Upstream and then again downstream, when we circled back, the river meandered—one astonishing bend pool after another, with pinched head, broadening current, undercut banks—some more than two feet back—and dark pools. And then there was another bend pool, one after the other, with fish everywhere you'd expect them to be.

Sandy used only a hair-wing Royal Wulff, #12, which he "could see," and I used only a Whitlock Hopper—to make some pretense at imitation.

The fish were from twelve to about eighteen inches, mostly browns, all wild, and the most generous, good-hearted, happy, well-fed, and properly brought up brown trout I had ever met. They made a certain sweet, bright splash and sucking sound when they rose—and they rose readily to the surface. They were fat trout with small heads. They either came in a fast rush to the dry fly at one of the spots Sandy said they'd be at, or we moved on. There was no fussing with these Blue Rock Creek trout.

We fished for three hours, quite leisurely, alternating so only one of us fished at a time and the other watched. The sock on my left foot slipped down under the ball of my foot and my heel began to rub roughly against my waders. I could tell that a slab of skin had been dislodged. At each step, the pain was raw and sharp. Sometimes I forgot it. Several times we caught three, four trout on as many casts.

Sandy counted.

We took fifty-five trout.

Now I have always wanted to say that I have just caught a preposterous number of trout—say, *thirty-eight*—but I always get bored counting at, say, three (and have rarely caught many more than that at one time anyway).

I caught a lot of trout that afternoon. I caught so many—for me—that I was prompted to think of Mr. Skues's story. Had I been in "the bad place"? Had I been given some glimpse of my hellish fate?

I could not think that. The fishing had been lovely—a freakishly good afternoon on an astonishing river—and by extension I could only think that more of it would be lovelier. Sandy did not look the worse for having fished every one of the last seventeen days on Blue Rock Creek, though I detected some slight disappointment that "the truly big ones" weren't active.

(Such, such are the minor diseases of privilege!)

Me? I could have taken another month of it. Two. Maybe more. I found not a thing hellish about that afternoon. It was close to perfect and not very challenging, and the companionship was good and the fish were happy and well brought up and they rose readily. . .

It was nearly perfect but not quite. The raw heel of my left foot pained me for a week. Maybe it was the pain, the friction, that saved me from Mr Skues's hell.

But I doubt it.

ON MY BRAVE WIFE

The other night, sitting with two fly-fishing friends, addicts both, who had come over to see my new seven-and-a-half-foot Kushner rod—an extraordinary instrument—I mentioned a trip I'd taken with my wife and oldest son to a remarkable valley in Colorado. My voice beginning to rise, I recalled the long haul over dirt roads, the frequent false trails we'd followed, following the briefest hint, from a friend's letter, that at the end of our trek we'd find one of those rare untrammeled corners of the trouter's world.

I have followed slenderer trails—and usually found less than I'd sought. It is the fisherman's way, exploring, and I shall follow such slim promises until I follow no more trails at all.

I spoke of that first sight of it—bright and silver through the trees, the river—after three hot summer hours on dusty roads; and of how we found a pleasant ranch along the bank, paid a modest rod fee (I had only enough money with me for one rod, so Paul and I would share), and went down to the water.

Mari came in with coffee, smiled, and stopped to listen patiently. My voice was quite shrill now, my eyes huge. Having made conspicuously little headway in interesting her, ever, in any matter piscatorial, I rarely allow the fevers to take me when she is present anymore. Still, we had found a happy truce. I lived that part of my life a bit more inwardly and she began to take her watercolors to riverbanks, perhaps because the mosquitoes seemed to bite less when she was working.

I knew she loved this valley. We'd spoken often of it. We'd even asked whether there might not be a few acres for sale, along the river. It is an isolated place, desolate for some, far from any town, far from any of the modern world's entertainments. One defiles such a valley by bringing anything but oneself. If one brings enough, the valley provides all else. Its long sloping and overlapping hills, spotted with small pine and hemlock, give way to broad, lush meadows; snow-blotched peaks reign at a great distance; cows grace the fields with their slow, heavy grace; and a bright dancing river runs through the heart of the place.

Peace. I'd never been to a place so peaceful.

Deep, quiet, lasting peace. Like a rare elixir.

Mari felt that way, too: I knew it.

In the winter, we learned, the snow was ten feet deep and the elk herds raided the cow barns; in late spring, the river was high, unfishable, but already the meadows were spotted yellow and purple with wildflowers. Then, in August, when we came, the waters came down and the river was a mecca: quick glides, riffles, bend pools studded with boulders and fallen trees. The water was emerald. The river was just small enough for the fly fisherman to touch its hiddenmost secrets, large enough for demanding casts and large trout. We saw no other fishermen along twenty miles of it.

And it was gorgeous.

"The whole valley was gorgeous, wasn't it, Mari?"

"Absolutely," she said with genuine enthusiasm. "I'd move there tomorrow."

Emboldened by her interest, I let my voice touch a wild note or two and went on to tell how Paul and I had gone upstream to the first great bend pool while Mari got out her watercolors. It was late afternoon and the valley was hushed. I was going to ask her to verify what happened next—how we'd seen a good trout turn in the current, fished for it with a Rio Grande King, taken it, taken three others in rapid succession, first Paul, then I, all fat wild rainbows, fourteen to eighteen inches—but I remembered suddenly, three years later, that Mari had not showed. We'd met her back at the car, after dark.

I squeezed my memory and it came up with roses: she hadn't been bitten to shreds by no-see-ums, there had been no visible scowls on her face, she'd seemed positively beatific.

At the time, I'd asked her nothing. Paul and I had been in a state of acute neurotic joy: we'd finally taken fifteen or so fish, all over fourteen inches, all spectacular jumpers. We'd never budged from our position just to the left of a boulder where the current broke and swirled. We'd said little. Mostly we'd smile when another fish rose and was properly struck, each turning to the other with an electric jerk, knowing and feeling together. His line went out more deftly with each cast; his reflexes were better than mine.

On the way back we relived it a dozen times, saw a slew of deer in the headlights, and were still in a trance when we returned to our cottage.

"Did they really get that many? That size?" one of my friends asked Mari. They were no worse than me: off the river, I rise regularly to such tales, demand proof and detail.

"Ask Paul," I said.

"He's just another fisherman. I asked Mari."

"They said so," she said.

"You didn't actually *see* it all?" the other asked. "There are rumors that Nick *never* catches any fish."

"They may be true," I muttered, taking back the Kushner and simulating a little side cast toward the pocket between the couch and the bookcase.

"No. I was busy," Mari said placidly.

"Painting?" I asked.

"No."

"You didn't spend the whole time in the car, did you? The sunset was incredible."

"No. I saw it. I got a good long look."

"Maybe *she* caught more trout herself, downstream," one of those jokers said, "and didn't want to embarrass you."

"Not hardly," she said, laughing.

"Well, what did you do?"

"If you must know," she said, "I got out my watercolors as I'd planned, went through the barbed-wire fence to the bank of the river, and sat down to work."

"I never saw that watercolor," I said. "I'd like a watercolor of that spot."

"I'd made a good start—a rather greenish landscape, of the river and some willows on the far bank, with a few cows off in the meadow, when I saw a black bull on my side of the water rear up, lower its head, and start toward me at a trot. I dropped half the paints, smeared the painting badly, and got behind the fence just in time. It was after me, all right. I ripped my dress and put a bad gash in my left ankle—"

"I don't remember a cut on your left ankle," I said.

"On fishing trips you don't often look at my left ankle. Anyway"—she was speaking in a perfectly normal, mild-mannered tone, and there was even a Madonna-like smile on her face—"I put the watercolors in the car and sat at the base of that huge rock hill a little downstream. You remember. The one about eighty feet high, of crushed boulders. The valley was exceptionally beautiful, so peaceful, and I was watching the way the hills changed color as the sun dropped, thinking of Turner, hoping you and Paul were having a good time—you'd dashed off so quickly I didn't have a chance to wish you good luck—when I saw something move out from one of the rock crevices just below me."

"Good grief."

"It was a snake. About six feet long." She held out hands, but they didn't go far enough. "Black. Making a rustling sound. Flicking its tongue. Slithering toward me."

"No!"

"Oh, yes. So I turned and scrambled right up that huge hill of rocks."

"You can't climb rocks!"

"You never saw anyone climb them faster. I shot up, bruising both knees, one elbow, my jaw, scratching my—"

"I never noticed," I said quite sheepishly.

"You never noticed!" said my friends, the Andrews sisters.

"It was dark when we got back," I explained.

"Anyway," Mari continued, her voice like honey, "I finally got to the top, looked back, almost fell down, and then turned at some noise and saw the hugest, shabbiest, fiercest wolf of a dog I've ever seen. It was growling in a low, steady growl and gnashing its huge teeth, and I almost fell down . . . where the snake was."

I couldn't say a word.

"That dog kept gnashing and growling for a full five minutes while I stood shivering with absolute terror on the tip of the rocks. Oh, yes. I could see clearly. All the time. The sunset was exceptional."

I looked at my friends. They were on the edges of their chairs.

"But then," Mari said, "a young boy came along."

I breathed deeply.

"He was quite young, but he was whittling on a stick with a ten-inch knife and looked like he'd come from the nearest reformatory—and he had the short butt of a cigar in the corner of his mouth, and his eyes . . ."

And the story went on, another ten minutes of it, interrupted by the chorus chanting "Peaceful valley!" "Brave woman!" "Brute."

When she was done, she smiled pleasantly and excused herself; she was rereading Henri Focilon on "The Life of Forms in Art."

My friends shook their heads in unison; they positively refused to look at my new fly rod, though I'd especially wanted them to feel how much more power the second, heavier, tip gave the rod. Finally, one of them said: "And she didn't say a thing until now? Three years later?"

"First I've heard of it," I said glumly, beginning to put the rod into its cloth bag.

"Remarkable."

"A brave, wise woman."

"All that ammunition and she's never used it. Jean would have . . ."

A few minutes later, they got up to leave. But first they went into the dining room where Mari, demurely, was reading.

Reverently, as if she was the sainted herald of a world that might be, they placed kisses upon the forehead of my brave wife.

I noticed, for the first time, she had a thin, white scar on the tip of her chin.

AN ORDINARY TRIP

We put in at the same place we had put in that other time, above Varney Bridge. I sat in the stern this time and Paul sat up front. Craig Mathews, who was guiding, walked the Mackenzie River boat—shaped like an old admiral's hat, inverted—out into the Madison River, and in a few moments, after the boat scraped with a raspy sound a few times against the rocks, we were floating.

I had my fly rod out at once and cast a Humpy backhanded off to the left. It perched high in the water and bobbed through a shallow and riffled run. We're in the domain of the sixty-foot drag-free float, I thought, and I watched the fly intently until the boat got too far below it, in faster current, and the fly dragged. Then I rolled the line off the water and again cast backhanded, across and a little upstream. I wanted to raise a good fish right away. It took the edge off if you got a trout right away. There was a certain pressure or tension at first on any trip. Would the water be right? Would the weather hold? Would the fish be working? Would the boats ahead of us—three had left in the past twenty minutes—have put the trout down? I wanted to get a fish, or even a good rise, at once, and then the pressure and the questions would be gone.

Later, when we came to that old spot, I could relax. I would not even fish. I wanted to see that particular channel very much. I wanted merely to look at it and to hold the images of that other trip against those of today—not as a yardstick but as something that might deepen the present, gild and layer it with the gold of the past. I had not spoken to Paul about it, about that other time, and I wondered if it was on his mind, too. He had been fourteen then and was now twenty-two. The halcyon years of his teens were over.

He was casting quite well from the bow and had picked up a few small fish, and Craig was saying that the water was a bit high —they were letting some water out of Hebgen Lake, and Craig theorized that this might stir up the big black stone-fly nymphs that were always in the river. That's what he'd use, he said: his version of the big black stone-fly nymph, probably with a bit of weight. Sometimes, he said, the release of water made the entire bottom of the river come alive.

In ten minutes we saw the last of the boats that had left before us and we stopped to let them work their way downstream. We beached the boat and fished the main flow without a strike, and then we all went off to the left, to fish one of the channels that broke out of the main river and rushed off and around a bend. I remembered how much I had enjoyed that other channel eight years earlier, how much it had reminded me of my eastern rivers, how generous it had been. It was more intimate than the big Madison and more fecund that afternoon than any river I had ever fished in the East. Fishing that tangled stretch of intertwining channels—breaking apart, twisting around a mound of rock and shrub, meandering—had been like discovering a rare hidden river.

We had beached the boat on a dry bar no more than forty feet from where the channel reentered the main river but had not seen the spot while we ate and talked. Then, after lunch, we had walked over and I knew immediately that it held fish. It was bright and alive, and when I waded into the shallows, two good brown trout darted twenty-five feet up and vanished in the wavering shadows of the riffle. I told Paul to rest the pool and I wandered upriver, where the channel became a maze of twists and bends and brushy undercut banks with angled, fallen trees and dark bend pools and snaky foam lines. From one of the foam lines, a brilliantly spotted wild brown trout rose with heavy speed and open mouth and nailed a Whitlock Hopper. A sight not to be forgotten. Nor the sight and feel of four more browns I took from those channels, which wandered and turned until they met and found their way back to the main river.

But what I remembered most about that day eight years earlier, what had stuck so sharply in my brain, was the sight when I came back around the last bend: Paul was standing on a bar near that first run, and his rod was bent perilously and he was a few minutes away from catching his first trout on a fly.

Craig and I got a few decent browns on Elk Hair Caddis at that first stop, and Paul had a few interesting strikes, and then, as we floated again, I kept thinking of that spot and of that day eight years earlier. We'll hit it at lunchtime, I thought, like the last time.

And so we floated and it was bright and warm and I watched Paul cast easily in against the bank and I watched his Blond Caddis float twenty, thirty feet, into pockets, under overslung shrubs, into little eddies. He took three rainbows, then a couple of browns, like he wanted to take them, on the top. I watched him and then spotted his fly, and then there would be a little splash and the fly would go under.

It was clear that the fish were not coming properly. I had fished the Madison enough to know that. So when we stopped again, Craig decided to use his big black stone-fly nymph, with a five-inch length of bright red yarn tied a couple of feet up from the fly, as an indicator. It's an unwieldy, atrocious-looking rig—but lethal. The fly, tied on a crimped hook, with a Swannundaze body and loose hackle for movement, is more than two inches long and weighted. Craig must have taken fifteen fish in a half-hour of rapid fishing, casting the awkward thing a short ways upstream, then following it down with his rod until the fly passed just a few feet out from him. Usually the strike came then. In a hard, fast run, Craig showed Paul how to use the thing and in the process—while I watched from a distance—raised an absolutely gigantic rainbow that swung up after the fly but struck short.

It had been an extremely pleasant trip so far, and it would become something special when we found that old spot. It ought to be soon now, I thought. It could not be much farther.

We kept taking only smaller fish on the top, so I—a bit greedily—switched to one of Craig's large nymphs; Paul, more a purist, stayed with dries. Then I hooked something that felt like an eight-pound brown—it got into a long heavy run and throbbed mightily; but it proved to be a three-pound whitefish hooked in the tail. Craig's stone flies were beautifully tied; I bummed five, and always glad to leave more in a river than I took, I left the streamside brush festooned with black stone-fly nymphs.

Craig was fine company for us. He had been a patrolman in Michigan and had come to West Yellowstone to be chief of police. On the side, he guided and tied flies and with his wife, Jackie, fished and hunted all year round. He told us about the enormous possibilities of the area, how much he fished, how well he had gotten to know the Madison in particular, and I felt envious as hell.

Did he know where the channel came in? It came in and went out in many places—what I described could be a dozen places.

We tried four but they were all wrong.

Was it so important to find that particular spot? Paul asked. Did it really matter?

We stopped again and then again and each time I looked

anxiously at the rocks and at the angle at which the channel entered the river. Each was different and none was the place I remembered.

Did it *really* matter? Paul asked. He was having a fine time, he said. It was a bright, warm day and he had taken off his shirt and caught a nice batch of fish on the dry fly to which he remained loyal, and he chided me lightly and wisely at my concern that he should hook a truly large fish and that we should find that old channel.

Maybe it was farther down, I thought. I watched the left bank intently as we floated and I saw nothing. Maybe the channels had shifted with the heavy rains or spring runoff. That must have happened. The channels had changed.

Well, Paul did not mind. He was a man now, with defined views on casting and dry-fly codes and the place of the big fish in one's pleasures, but he was not nearly old enough—quite clearly —for sentimentality, the disease of middle age.

Perhaps it didn't matter, I thought as the skies suddenly changed and a wind came up and within minutes a summer squall moved in. It had been quite an ordinary day, without a truly big fish and without a speck of gold from the past. But when we all piled into Craig's pickup, after taking out just above Ennis, and settled in for the long ride back to West Yellowstone, I happened to notice that we were all smiling.

Maybe there was a message in that.

ON THE BEACH

LEFTY AND ME

There is a photograph of the great Lefty Kreh holding up a gargantuan tarpon. Lefty is straining and smiling while with both hands he grips the rope of a flying gaff whose point protrudes from the huge fish's lower jaw. The tarpon—so vast a fish that only its head and a quarter of its body show in the picture—must be six or seven feet long, perhaps 120 pounds. Lefty's huge barrel chest is prominent.

"So that's what saltwater fishing is all about," I thought when I first saw the picture. "And on a fly! What an event."

Preston Jennings found saltwater fly fishing "too athletic," but Sparse tells me that George LaBranche, in his last years, forwent the pleasures of a dry fly in fast water for the lure of fast bonefish on the flats. Frank Woolner, that sweet, crusty surf-fishing master, whetted my interest in the salt, and then so did Art Flick, with tales of snook and trout and tarpon fishing down south. And the late Charles Ritz, at a luncheon in New York City, positively rose from the table and shouted to me when I asked him about saltwater fly fishing: "Ahhh. It is only for the strong man with a hard stomach. It is like sex after lunch!"

He was past eighty at the time.

So I began to dream of gigantic tarpon, leaping snook, savage bluefish, of tussles that made my arms ache and my stomach collapse. Lyons against anything that roamed the sea! Against stripers, barracuda, dogfish, redfish, permit, anything. Against white sharks, sperm whales, even!

Yes. I'd try it. I'd grown a soft belly but I'd been athletic enough in my salad days; I could stand it. I could stand a dose of such monsters very comfortably, indeed.

So I began to take a heavy fly rod for a #8 line with me whenever I knew I'd be within ten miles of a beach. I even bought a batch of huge saltwater poppers to go with the Lefty's Deceivers the master himself had given me.

But for several years I never uncased the rod. The wind was bad, the boat's motor conked out, the fish were too far offshore.

Then, last summer, I managed to engineer a three-week vacation on the island of Martha's Vineyard, off lower Cape Cod, and vowed: I will not leave this place until I take a blue on the fly rod.

Strong words. Determined words. The words of a man who will do what he says.

I had a very clear image of an evening, four years earlier, when the blues were careening back and forth along Lobsterville Beach near Gay Head, so close I could flick a cigar butt out and they'd slash at it. I'd take them. A dozen. Two dozen perhaps. And right from the shore.

I fitted my largest fly reel with more than one hundred yards of twenty-pound-test Dacron, triple-tested the knot joining flyline to backing—making sure it was not only firm but would slip through the guides smoothly—and bought a coil of single-strand wire to make into three-inch shock tippets.

When the blues did not show the first evening, I was scarcely troubled. I still had nearly three weeks: they'd be in, and I'd be ready. To prepare myself, I decided I'd better practice casting. So one night, while everyone else was merrily flinging three-ounce plugs and catching nothing, I decided I'd just as well catch nothing with my fly rod.

I rigged up carefully, clipped off my leader to about seven feet, attached the wire and then the fly, and got a tremendous shock: I couldn't cast the thing ten feet. Now, I've seen movies of Lefty casting a saltwater fly, and it's obviously as easy as tossing a ball. The long line goes back effortlessly, there's a double tug, and then the line shoots out and out . . . and out. I had resigned myself to half, maybe a quarter that distance, but not this. I'd juggled the pacing of my cast with a bass bug, but I'd never had this problem. The huge popper jerked back like an apple on a string, dropped, hooked upward, turned in a gigantic, flopping motion when I brought it forward, and collapsed on the surface. It was not a graceful affair.

I tried harder.

The results were worse.

I tried to let the line lengthen more slowly behind me, to let the popper straighten before pushing it forward. A bit better but not much. I clipped my leader back to *three* feet: it was thick enough to spook a Battenkill brown a mile upstream. Now the big popper straightened more easily behind me, rolled out with fewer somersaults.

Still not far enough. Without the double-haul, without an even heavier rod, I was quite doomed not to be able to reach any fish that did not seriously want to feed close enough for me to spit on its dorsal fin. And the wind? It made bird's nests of even my best efforts. And the whole affair was positively dangerous: that 2/0 hook came winging past my ears and jugular, slammed into my sunglasses once, whacked me on the back so hard I thought I'd been shot.

So I put my long rod away and waited and watched. Each day I went to the beach with my children and looked for birds working, for some disturbance on the water that would indicate feeding fish close to shore. I listened for reports. I checked the tackle shops every day. Nothing. The fish weren't in. No one knew where they were.

Then, several days before we had to leave, I spotted some kids on a dock catching an occasional snapper blue—baby bluefish perhaps six inches long—on spinning rods. I'd caught snappers at Sheepshead Bay when I was their age, dozens of them on a cane pole and frozen spearing. Perhaps. It was better than nothing, and I could surely use my fly rod.

I bought some small freshwater streamers with Mylar or tinsel bodies, rebuilt my leader to eight feet, with a 3X tippet, and began to explore.

In Menemsha, where the Pond fed into a channel and washed into the bight, there was a strong current on either the incoming or outgoing tide; the wind was minimal. If you squinted, the moving water looked exactly like a river; and if you looked closely, you could find little eddies, backwaters, and breaks in the steady flow where snappers might hold, where bait fish—buffeted by the tidal surge—might cluster. I slipped on my waders and sloshed to within forty feet of one such hole.

For years I have followed the Numbers Game with morbid fascination: this expert caught forty-three trout in two hours, that one got twenty-seven at dusk. Were I ever by wild chance to catch more than five at one time, I'm sure I'd lose count. I fish for fun, not to improve my mathematical skills. But I caught a hundred, maybe two hundred snappers in the next few days. There was action on every cast. Four, five of the silver-blue darters would lunge at the fly, hit it once, twice, three times before they hooked themselves. They tore the half dozen streamers to shreds, to the bare hook, with only a few strands of impala or squirrel tail holding desperately to the shank; they chewed up three bluegill poppers—leaping over each other to get up at them. What savage beasts! They rose and charged and swirled and ganged up on every fly I cast to them—and they were just where trout might have been, in the eddies and breaks. Pound for pound—though they were admittedly only six or seven to the pound—they were the scrappiest, snappingest fish this side of the piranha, even if they took me nowhere near my backing. Anthony, my thirteen-year-old, got a dozen and a half one evening—on flies: and they taught him as much about fly rodding as bluegills had once taught me. We brought a batch of them home that night and we fried them like smelt, dipped in beaten eggs and rolled in bread crumbs, and they were delicious.

All in all, I was feeling very damned happy with myself—having caught *something*; having caught my first saltwater fish on flies; having surely caught more fish per hour than *anyone*, ever—until I thought of Lefty's tarpon, a photo I once saw of Mark Sosin with a huge fly-caught permit, and a movie of Lee Wulff whopping a couple-of-hundred-pound marlin on a fly rod.

Snappers!

Well, I might have said, had I been pressed, that I'd caught several hundred bluefish. They *were* bluefish.

I'd had great fun—which I always have when I fish—but as usual it really didn't add up to very much. I could even have fished for these bluefish after lunch without much of a twinge in my stomach.

Always prepared, I'd asked my daughter Jennifer to follow me around with a camera. She got one memorable photograph of me smiling and straining to release a bluefish approximately six inches long, seven to the pound, fly-caught. The sunset is gorgeous. My barrel belly is prominent. The fish doesn't show.

GORILLA BLUES

You are a fly fisherman and you live on the East Coast and you are planning next summer's vacation already. Along with Montana and Labrador and Alaska and Maine and upper Michigan and Canada and Yugoslavia, consider East Hampton, which is most of the way out on Long Island—that is, pretty far out. If you are a fly fisherman, consider East Hampton very carefully.

By some cunning logic that I don't quite understand, I was led to forgo any western or northern forays from my beloved New York City and persuaded that to the east lay salvation, or at least a place where a tired old fellow could get a bit of sun and sand, where there were no blackflies—and why shouldn't I bring along my fly rod, because the blues were right in the breakers the last time we went, when I fished with a surf-casting rod.

Now I have never caught a bluefish on a fly rod, and though I'm not particularly a thrill-seeker in my fly-fishing life, I rather fancied it would be a good thing to do once or twice. So I took along my surf equipment and added a #8 graphite fly rod, a reel with one hundred yards of twenty-pound-test backing, some skipping bugs and saltwater poppers and a few Lefty's Deceivers and this and that large enough to interest a big bluefish. My friend Peter Chan told me there were some huge largemouth black bass in Fort Pond, in Montauk, so I could surely catch some of those if the blues were dining elsewhere; the bass would surely think highly of some new Whitlock bass bugs I brought along.

With such Great Expectations dancing like sugarplums in my brain, I braved the Long Island Expressway for five hours, noted to Mari that we could have been in Montana already (to which she replied: "Or the south of France!"), and finally arrived at that mecca of literary and artistic aristocracy, East Hampton, just as the annual Artists and Writers Game (of softball) was breaking up. The town itself looked like a dozen other chic-chic spas I've seen (why do towns always look alike to me, trout streams different?) and was so crammed we drove through it six times looking for a place to park, found none, then headed further east, and finally found a comfortable little motel that might have been used as a prop in *Psycho*. Maybe the similarity was why it cost only the price of a good graphite rod to spend the night.

I immediately read all the local newspapers, looking for fish news. Frank Mundus had wrestled in a gigantic shark the week before; bushels of "jumbo porgies" were being hauled in every day; the "gorilla blues" had not yet hit the beaches but were expected hourly. "Gorilla." Ah, the happy garish extravagance of fish talk! I checked the tide charts, readied my gear, and went to the four or five tackle shops between Sag Harbor and Montauk, to get the best local advice on these monsters.

I have been few places in this world where I could not find a little serious fly-fishing talk. In Paris, in London, in San Francisco, let alone Roscoe or West Yellowstone or Manchester, Vermont, one need only mention "a number twenty-two Trico" under one's breath and half the room grows quiet and listens. If you are planning a fly-fishing trip to East Hampton, bring along a fly-fishing friend or a cassette, for no one within thirty miles of the place has heard of fly fishing. At least I could not find such a person. I mentioned the Trico a few times quietly and raised no one; I shouted; I tried to buy some snapper flies in one shop and was asked if I meant sand fleas. Most had never heard of a fly; those who had, thought I was a lunatic, and surely not a good candidate to buy a dozen six-dollar Striper Swipers and some four-ounce surgical tube lead-head eel rigs.

If you truly believe, deep down, that fly fishing is a loner's game, you'll find no better place to practice it than East Hampton.

Normally, this lack of a fly-fisherman's ambiance, the lack of talk, the absence of local knowledge about fly-fishing possibilities, would have discouraged me. It did not. Let the Artists play the Writers, I thought, I'd play Johnny Appleseed and plant the seeds of fly fishing in that barren chic-chic turf.

I began by lying in the sun an hour too long, deliberately, and burning my legs to a crisp; I was now quite unable to sit with my wife on the beach and was forced to explore other vacation options. Every morning at six I went down to the breakers and cast out my Striper Swiper; as soon as I caught a blue, knew they were in, I'd switch to the fly rod and zap one of those gorillas. Now and again I saw some birds dip and dart, but if there were gorilla blues in the area, they did not come to my plug, nor to my Hopkins lure, nor to some surgical tubing the length of nine Lefty's Deceivers laid end to end. I caught nothing. I had not one strike. I saw one other fisherman, who was casting with his spinning reel *above* the rod, and that did not augur well.

In Montauk, as I began to explore all possibilities, I saw signs at the docks proclaiming that those Jumbo Porgies, Giant Cod, Gigantic Fluke, and Gorilla Blues could be caught from party boats. I had no desire to pioneer fly fishing for cod in sixty feet of water, and the Gorillas could only be caught on the night shift, on diamond jigs, which (at six ounces) were heavier than my fly rod.

I tried Fort Pond vigorously for a couple of hours, but the bass had never seen a Most-Whithair Bug and couldn't pronounce it and never showed.

I tried the bay side of the island and discovered a channel where Gardiners Bay flowed into a large lake. An elderly lady was fishing deftly with a spinning rod and a Johnson Spoon, and she claimed to have caught half a dozen fluke, a couple of one-pound blues, and a seventeen-inch weakfish right there in the channel. That sounded promising, so I rigged up my fly rod and immediately was into a fine five-inch snapper that did not take me into the backing, and I caught a dozen more and vowed to come back when the tides were better but never did. The lady had the right method—and I had begun to doubt, after four hours of casting, that a self-respecting gorilla blue would come into such tame waters.

By the end of the week I'd caught thirty snappers, no fluke, no more sunburn, and no big blues. I went back to Montauk and at Gosman's Dock, near that wonderful seafood restaurant, saw that the tide was sweeping in and I might as well make my last stand—a kind of Custer of the Little Big Hampton. Others were there before me. A young man was fishing with a spin-casting outfit, rigged with a popping device in front of a small rubber eel lure. He cast far out into the channel and retrieved lickety-split. Most times, reeling without stop, a silver-blue snapper would suddenly appear, splashing, hooked to the little eel lure. Half the snappers went into the bucket; the others found themselves promptly cut in half and used as fluke bait by an older brother who could cast his surf rig a country mile; the brother nearly caught a gorgeous cabin cruiser called *Poverty Stinks* and got three small fluke. Another fellow used bits of clam and was collecting some yummy little flounder the size of flapjacks and some ugly creatures I recognized as sea robins. The latter did not seem suitable fly-rod quarry, so I took my best option to be the snappers, which I soon began to catch on a small white streamer. I got a couple in ten or twelve casts, and some light taps, while the kid—with minor exceptions—caught one on every cast.

Not to compete but in the spirit of innovation, I thought like a snapper (or a snapper fisherman) and tied on a cork bass popper with a streamer eight inches back, as a dropper. As with the kid's rig, the popper would attract them, the streamer would catch them. This minor tactic for channel fishing on Montauk Point I considered genius.

With the wind at my back and the spade hackle on the bass bug acting as a kite, I cast a full flyline for the first time in my life and then looked around to see if anyone was watching this miraculous feat. No one was. They were watching the pursuit of sea robins and the two-hundred-foot casting feats of the surf-caster; they were eating lobster and clams; they considered me a lunatic, who caught a Wagoneer on a backcast and created bird's nests when a cast collapsed in tangles during a shift of the wind. Finally I sent one far into the backing and began a rapid strip retrieve that left my left hand feeling as if it had got caught in a vibrating machine. After three or four such retrieves, my stripping hand was lifeless and I simply sat back quietly to watch the spin-casting genius take his eighty-third and eighty-fourth snapper routinely. At least it was better than sitting on the beach.

The trip back to the city took a neat six hours, in blinding rain. Three days later I had a dream about a gorilla blue, woke and checked my fly reel, and found it ruined from the salt.

Yes, give some serious thought to taking your fly rod to East Hampton on your next vacation; then leave it home—or head for Alaska.

A SNOOK FOR CHRISTMAS

We must have wanted a Christmas in Florida badly, or perhaps Christmas wanted us, for the day we arrived on Captiva Island so did raw winds, rain, and the threat of frost. The Sunshine State was gray; it was cold enough to snow. We weren't sure whether to cry or leave and settled for three whiskey sours at the Mucky Duck.

Jack Koontz, a fledgling thirty-year-old guide we'd met on Martha's Vineyard—and liked enormously—had urged us to come. He was guiding on Captiva for the winter, and his reports about the beauty of the island, the fine shells to be found, and the fish he'd been catching were sorely tempting. Besides, Jack was lucky and you go with luck. On the first day he guided at Martha's Vineyard he and a party of three men from Boston found a school of migrating striped bass and bluefish gorging themselves on menhaden. In four hours they boated nine bass, the largest forty-eight pounds, and twenty bluefish, two of which went seventeen pounds. They were all taken on the surface. When a man is lucky like that you stay near him, especially when he writes that he and Doug Fischer, a seasoned Captiva guide, had found a secluded pond where they caught and released twenty-four snook one afternoon.

Snook. The fish began to haunt me as Mari and I drove south. We'd made all our plans the evening before, jumped into the old Mercury wagon, and raced from winter. Mari thought we were going for the sun; I was on the trail of snook. Our children were scattered for the holidays and we would miss a Christmas at home for the first time in eighteen years—without a tree, without those carefully selected and wrapped presents—but perhaps we'd find something in the sun. Snook. Art Flick had told me about them; he fished for them with streamers and poppers on the mideastern coast of Florida. He compared them to brown trout—wary, selective, hard-fighting —and by the look in his eye when he spoke of them, I knew I could easily lose my heart to the fish with the funny name. Mari liked the name "robalo" better, especially when I rolled the r. Robalo—of the razor gill. Robalo—lover of tangled mangroves. I intended, without fail, to get me a snook for Christmas.

I had to settle for the whiskey sours that first bleak day on Captiva, when the temperature dropped to the high thirties and the winds gusted up to thirty miles per hour. You could not fish from the shore and you could not put a boat, even Jack's sturdy Aquasport, on water so choppy. "Do you think we brought this weather?" asked Mari. "We managed to bring a hurricane to Martha's Vineyard."

"Probably," I said. "But I'm still going to get me a robalo."

Two days later the rains stopped, the winds dropped to only fifteen miles per hour, and there were patches of sun. Jack said the snook would be too deep, in deep-water holes, but the sea trout might be along the edges of the weed beds. We tried for them for an hour, and Jack got two, several pounds each, but the wind made casting difficult and Mari was huddled so far into her down jacket that I thought she was hibernating. We settled this time for a long lunch at Cabbage Key, a very special place with hills of shells the early Indians had stacked, and a restaurant with a screened porch shaded by a mammoth Cuban laurel with twenty trunks. Since the winds were still strong, Jack took us to an isolated beach he'd found, with extraordinary shells. We found scallops and oozing sea urchins that would dry into domes like Byzantine mosques, and starfish, whelks, unbroken sand dollars, a huge horse conch, tulips, banded tulips, fighting conchs, and a lovely apple murex—almost more than we could carry in our arms and pockets to the boat. On the way back we saw a strip of sand crammed with the rare white pelicans and then were treated to a glimpse of three porpoises making tooled and rhythmic rolls.

But no snook.

From Timmy's Nook we saw a gill-netter bring up thirty of them along with mullet and sheepshead and a few trout. They were beautiful fish, the first snook I'd ever seen—with backs of green-gold, bright silver bodies, a sharply tapered snout, and that famous long, curved lateral stripe. "I'm going to get me a snook for Christmas," I told Mari, "if I have to stay here until June."

"I'll settle for a new suit, wrapped, with a ribbon, under a tree," Mari said. "I miss our tree."

Friday the 24th was raw, gray, and windy at the start, so Mari slept late and I bundled up and went out with Jack. Within an hour the skies opened, the winds died, the sun blazed down on us, and I caught my first bluefish on a fly—about two pounds, arrogantly strong for its size. Jack said that no one threw back blues but it would be a nice gesture to do so with my first caught on a fly; I readily did so—and later that day also returned the first sea trout I caught on a fly, a small shiny one that came to one of Jack's yellow streamers, tied on a Keel Hook. He calls the fly the Koontz Self-deceiver. It worked as well for trout as it had for bluefish— and I enjoyed drifting along that shallow weed bed, casting the fly far ahead of us and retrieving it in short tugs.

"Any chance of snook?" I asked.

Jack said the tide was wrong and that they were in the deep holes. When the weather warmed, they'd come into the mangroves and you could take them when the falling tide began to sweep baitfish out. The sea, which had seemed so vast and incomprehensible to me, was becoming—like the streams and lakes I knew—a *lawful* place. Jack said he was still learning—there was so much to learn and only Lefty Kreh knew it all—but "change" seemed the best place to start. Fish fed on changing tides, where baitfish became vulnerable; sea trout were in the darker areas of the bay, where the sandy bottom changed to patches of weed bed; redfish were at the points of mangrove outcroppings, where the tides caused swirls and eddies; bluefish—as everywhere—were under the birds. You had to look for signs, changes; you had to learn to read the tides and contours of the bottom. The sea began to make a bit of sense.

Christmas day broke raw and windy again, and we slept late and talked about trees and presents, and I gave Mari a little shell necklace. All I wanted, I told her, was a snook. "Maybe," she said, "there are no robalo who care to become your Christmas present."

"It does look like a grim, gray Christmas," I said.

We met Jack after lunch, and miraculously, the sun broke

through, the winds calmed again, and he said we'd be able to try that little pond he and Doug Fischer had found, connected to the bay by a narrow canal. We could just catch the falling tide and there was a good chance we'd catch us some snook for Christmas.

The pond was no more than a jagged half-acre, quite deep and nearly surrounded by tangled mangroves. Mari found a patch of sand near a clump of towering old palm trees and lay down to take the sun. The air was warm now, in midafternoon, and there was no wind. It was a beautiful spot.

Restless and a bit overanxious, I wandered down the canal, which was narrow and overhung with mangroves, casting the Koontz Self-deceiver on a short line and drawing it back with quick little stripping tugs. Nothing. I tried to think like a snook but had to admit that I had no idea how a snook thought. Still nothing. And nothing at the broad pool where two canals met; and nothing on the way back to the pond. I tried a bass bug and some freshwater streamers and even a large wet fly, but these were clearly outside any self-respecting snook's canon of thought.

When I got back to the pond, I saw that Jack had taken one, a fine five-pounder, and he was thrilled with it.

"Your turn," he said, and told me to cast across the pond, up as close as I could to the overslung mangroves. My new double-haul worked—after a fashion—and I managed three or four casts to within a foot of the brush. "Even closer if you can," Jack whispered. "They'll lie right up in the roots and hanging branches. And let the fly sink for a second or two before you start your retrieve." I did so. On the third cast, the line stopped, I felt the telltale tug, there was a roll on the surface, and I had my first snook on a fly.

That my robalo was the size of most trout I caught bothered me not a whit. I smiled bright as the bright sun in the Christmas sky. I avoided the razor gills, slipped the Self-deceiver from the fish's jaw, and gently returned it to the pond.

"You got your robalo," Mari said.

"Fairly, on a fly," said Jack.

"Wrapped in silver, with a long lateral ribbon," I said, still smiling, "for Christmas."

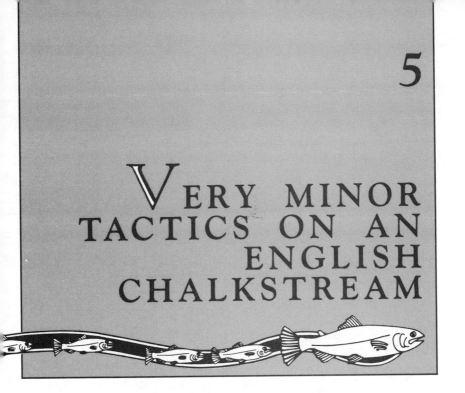

5

VERY MINOR TACTICS ON AN ENGLISH CHALKSTREAM

THE FASCINATION OF WHAT IS DIFFICULT

"How do you cast?" I asked, eyeing the row of coarse high weed in front of me, the low-branched maple behind my right shoulder. Beyond the weeds I could still see, if barely, the vague form of the brown trout; it was two feet downstream from where the slight riffle broke, raised up into midwater, feeding. It was not small.

If my backcast was perfect—no more than four feet above the ground, with a tight loop, and if I could then just lift it slightly above the weed, and then shoot just enough line—I might possibly get a foot of clear float before the fly came over the trout. But I would have to snake the line a little. And hook it a little to the left. And I would have to turn the line over at just the right moment. And I was kneeling, on both knees, stretching high to see over the weed, then bending to get low enough to backcast under the branches. I do not cast precisely like a dream while standing and doubted if a cast from this position would be much better than a nightmare. My son Anthony was watching from behind the left side of the tree. No; I could not possibly hook *him*. Brian was safely farther left. They were watching me intently. I did not especially want to flub this cast, too.

What to do?

I had already spent ten minutes playing Toulouse-Lautrec, knee-walking, ever so slowly, to this position. The trout had not spooked yet, but I did not think I could chance another movement. I would get one cast, perhaps two. "How the blazes do you *cast?*" I asked again, in a hoarse whisper.

"With great difficulty," said Brian, a second before my backcast reached tentatively behind me, straightened, and did not come forward. It had happened like that twice before that morning; it would happen several more times before the day was done.

I was on the "Wilderness" section of the Kennet—exquisite water, perhaps the choicest in England—with Brian Clarke and John Goddard, two of Britain's finest chalkstream fishermen. It was my first day on a chalkstream, and I was being instructed—by friend and ritual and circumstance—in the fascination of what is difficult. Fascination, not frustration. Challenge, not futility.

The fish were there. Dozens of them. As we walked cautiously along the bank of the main stem and then up the smaller, clearer carriers, we could see them—fine, nearly wild brown trout in the two- to three-pound class. Brian, in the morning, and then John, always saw them first; then, following the line of a finger, peering into water as clear as that in a glass, I would catch a hint, a motion, a break in the color, and there it would be, a brightly spotted trout, facing upstream, moving on occasion to one side or the other, always wary.

I had always prided myself on my eyes. I had begun to fish on hard-pounded public rivers, and I had learned to read water because that was the only way you had a chance to take a decent fish. When I had heard, before we started out that morning, that on British chalkstreams one was expected to cast upstream with a floating line and had to fish, always, to a sighted fish, I had thought these quaint, arbitrary customs. I was willing, in England, to do as my English friends did, but I could not quite believe the code was more than an antiquated ritual, an amusingly perverse way of making a simple, lovely pastime outrageously complex. Even impossible.

"This is tough fishing, Dad," Anthony whispered to me a few times as he trudged along with us bravely, without a rod, watching, hoping I would get at least one fish.

"Too tough for me, old man," I said.

"But you're a famous fisherman," he said. "You don't want to go a whole day with these guys and not catch anything. It's humiliating."

"I've made my reputation on precisely that," I said. I said it quietly. "Anyway, it's more fun when it's hard. Isn't it?"

"I think it's fun to catch fish," he said.

After I had spooked four trout before I saw them, I realized that I was unprepared for this sort of game, out of my league. I was even tempted once, when I was alone, to shuffle out a little downstream cast—may the gods forgive me—but got a good, honorable hold on myself in time.

Yet after I had followed Brian's finger and then John's a dozen times, out over the high weed and down into some pellucid run, I realized that the laws were not merely arbitrary. I could justify them *aesthetically*—for these waters. I could also justify them as restrictions that drew forth abilities admirably suited to such demanding rivers. Brian and John had learned to *see* trout before trout saw them, just as I had once learned to read water. Shadows, hints of shadows, the slight opening of a trout's mouth, the undulating movement of its body, the minutest break in the prismic fabric of the water, the rose moles on a fish's back—these and a dozen other muted, subtle sights had of necessity become telltale hieroglyphs to these men. They saw with a finer eye, walked with gentler tread, had learned to make every cast count. No Halford purists, they had championed upstream nymph fishing, with shrimp imitations and the butt of the leader greased to announce the take; they were innovative and maverick but within the basic parameters of a difficult code that contained a built-in beauty as well as a built-in challenge. They loved this fishing especially for its difficulty.

And so, as the day wore on, did I.

Not that I managed it with even rudimentary skill; not that I managed even to move *one* of those fine, wary trout: it was *too* difficult for me that first day, a bit beyond my skill of hand or eye. Oh, Brian and John tried. They found fish for me in open water and in narrow channels. They dazzled me with what they saw that I could not see. We meandered with the river, talking quietly, becoming closer friends, watching—always watching the water. Often we would go ten or fifteen minutes before we saw a trout. ("More walking and looking than fishing," Anthony said.) Then, intensely, one of us would stalk a fish, work ever so slowly into position, make one or two or perhaps three casts before the fish scooted off. They provided the proper flies, nymphs and shrimp of their own design. They even took several fish apiece before the long glorious day was over, perhaps to convince me that it could be done. ("Why don't *you* ever get one?" asked Anthony.) But I went skunked. Curiously, I was humbled but not frustrated; my imagination was piqued by it all, not turned off. I had, after all, learned immensely; my pleasure, and it was of the rarest sort, was quite independent from fish catching.

Don Zahner once advised me: "You're downgrading yourself too much, Nick. You're not nearly so bad a fisherman as you make out." I didn't mind the faint praise then, the backhanded compliment; and since that advice I have sincerely tried to catch a few fish now and then, not merely play the lunatic bumbler along the streams that touch my heart. The humbling I felt that day was a good rung or two above the embarrassment I usually feel. Without self-irony, I can report it frankly. There was no dishonor to not catching fish in the Kennet in high summer when no fish were rising. There was only an increasing fascination with what was difficult—crystalline water, wary trout, tough casts, an exacting ethic. When dark came, I was as exhausted and shivering from the intensity of this thing as I'd have been had I taken a truly monstrous trout. And in the car heading back to London, I vowed that as I grew older, I would value, more and more, fishing that is choice and hard.

Later that week I fished Dermot Wilson's water on the Test and fared somewhat better. It was not easy fishing—at least not for me—but the fish were quite large and I was, frankly, delighted to take a few from such genial, storied water. Even then, though, I envied an English companion who quietly passed up the open water there and fished a minute nymph seventy feet across stream, across braided currents, and took some smaller but quite difficult fish against the far bank. He could not resist the greatest challenges any more than I could resist, that day, taking a few fish.

It is rumored that Dermot helped Anthony "in some small way" to catch that huge brown trout the boy kept safely for three hours for me to see. The fish was perhaps five pounds, handsomely formed, with a sharply hooked jaw and gigantic red spots. Anthony thought it even larger, and indeed it has grown in his reports of that day to eight, ten, and now even twelve pounds.

"It wasn't *that* hard," Anthony said nonchalantly, when he finally released a fly-caught brown larger than any I have ever taken. "It gave a terrific fight; it ran all over the place; but I finally got it. I could have taken ten more like that and not minded. It couldn't be too easy for me. I wouldn't have been bored. I *like* to catch big fish."

I watched the huge trout waver heavily on its side, turn back up, and at last glide off. Anthony was full of pride at his catch, regretting that he could not haul it around with him for the next six months and show it to all his New York chums. I thought of my friend who chose to fish the toughest stretch of the Test, of John and Brian and their hawk's eyes; I thought that someday I would grow young enough again to feel Anthony's delight and wise enough to take a truly difficult trout.

VERY MINOR TACTICS ON AN ENGLISH CHALKSTREAM

An English chalkstream is a gentle, pastoral part of this frantic world. Limpid green and translucent, the river glides clear and steadily over flowing waterweed. Here and there a swallow or marten or finch dips and glides. Herefords graze in the lush meadow. Protected for centuries, guarded by riverkeeper and rule and club fiat, the water and its world are much like they were a thousand years ago. Yet on such gentle waters, within the frame of carefully fashioned codes, mighty dramas often transpire.

From a busy week in London, an American went one morning recently to the "Wilderness" section of the River Kennet in Berkshire, one of the noblest of the chalkstreams. The Kennet, carefully tended by the good riverkeeper Bernard, grows lusty trout to test the highest art of skilled fly fishers. John Goddard, who has taken three- and four-pound brown trout from these noble waters, usually passes the stern test. The American could not have had a better guide. And he had the company of Timothy Benn to advise him wisely about tactics.

The American had been to this river before. He had fished the Kennet several years earlier, for twelve hours. There were good trout in the Kennet—two- and three-pound browns—and he had seen many of them that day. You had to be careful to see the fish before the fish saw you, and the fish should be "on the fin," feeding. That was the code. You fished to the fish; you did not fish the water. And you fished only upstream, with a floating line. Often you had to kneel so that the trout would not see you, and the American marveled later that he had spent most of that day in the praying position, although, perhaps mistakenly, not for spiritual guidance. Often the casts had to be guided with deft skill through the maze of low branches, back branches, and high border weeds; the American only sometimes managed this but felt his flies lent a festive touch to the trees. And the trout spooked easily. The American had not gotten one of those large Kennet browns to move toward one of his flies.

But for two years he had dreamed of the river, and his dreams were mingled with the most cunning scheming. This time he was not without strategies. He had studied the minor tactics. He had learned the puddle cast. And he carried his lucky net.

But then, that morning, working hard and fishing to two or three good trout on the fin, he'd moved precisely no fish. He was not up to it. It was my youth, he thought in a paroxysm of shame, misspent worming and spinning. I am unworthy. And there is too little time to train the eye and hand for such noble work, let alone cleanse the soul.

The three had a pleasant lunch near the river, drank some

wine, ate pâté, laughed, told tales, and then headed out again. Neil Patterson, a young friend who lived on the river and would meet them later, had left a map for the American indicating that in the upper region there were some "very interesting trout." It was good, the American thought, to know young men who knew interesting trout.

The wine had been cool and pleasant and the American had perhaps drunk a glass too much of it, which made three. He did not count as one of his very few virtues the ability to drink much wine or to remember the names of the wines he had drunk. They all sounded French. The afternoon was warm and he had eaten well and he had had that extra glass of wine, and he was feeling very content and hopeful when John Goddard spotted a steadily rising fish of about two pounds at the head of a broad pool. This proved to be a most interesting trout. Despite two slap casts, three linings, and an hour of more delicate work, the fish was still rising merrily to naturals with very slow, very deliberate rises. He is lunching at Simpson's, the American thought, and he has paid a pretty ten pounds sterling for the privilege and he will not be disturbed by the traffic on the Strand or the punk-rock crowds at the Lyceum. He is quite intent on the business at hand and knows precisely what he has ordered.

So the American was pleased when John Goddard called downstream, "When you've had enough of him, come up here. I've spotted an interesting fish." Timothy Benn, who had taken a fine two-pounder that morning, positioned himself upstream with a camera to record properly the confrontation of the American with this new interesting trout.

The fish was feeding in a one-foot eddy behind a knobby root on the opposite side of the river. The American knew that the fish would not move an inch from that spot any more than the Simpson's trout would be disturbed at his selective lunching. He knew that an exceptional cast was needed—upstream, with some particular loops of slack, in close to the bank—for the fly to catch the feeding lane and float into the trout's dining room without drag. A puddle cast.

After four short casts and another two that led to drag, the American was sure he could not manage this minor tactic. It was subtler fishing than he was used to, and he was not impressed with his ability to move Kennet trout. But he had not put it down. The occasional sip-rises in the eddy continued. The fish might be quite large.

And the American managed an able puddle cast beyond his wildest hopes and the fly floated a foot or two and went calmly into the trout's domain, and he heard someone whisper, "He'll come this time," and miracle of miracles, the trout did.

The trout rose, was hooked, made a low jump, came clear of the stump and then streaked downstream, its back bulging the surface, its force bending the bamboo rod sharply. A very good fish. Better than two pounds.

From that point on, the American was not sure why he acted the way he did. Perhaps it was that he had just read something about getting below a fish, which proved that fishermen should read fewer books. Perhaps it was the extra glass of wine. More likely it was pure panic.

The American bolted. He began high-stepping downriver, busting, bursting the pastoral quiet of the chalkstream with his wild splashes. He heard one of his companions, in a high, incredulous, voice ask: "*Where* are you going?"

The trout, which had never witnessed a performance like this, and considered it extremely poor form, raced farther from the area in sheer embarrassment.

Then the American did something else he later could not explain. With the trout still green, he grasped for his lucky net.

The net was of the teardrop variety and had been bought in the Catskills and treasured for many years. The American carried it loose in his ArctiCreel, where it was safe from the brush. In fact, only a half-hour earlier he had advised his English friends that this was a much more suitable net than the long-handled nets they carried, and that it could be carried in the creel, safe from the brush, out of harm's way, until needed.

The American grasped the handle of the net and wrestled it from his creel. In so doing, out came his fly box. This was his prized fly box, a Wheatley, the most expensive kind of Wheatley, with compartments on both sides, and he had filled it for this trip with some of his choicest flies—flies by Flick and Troth and Whitlock and Leiser.

The fly box twisted in the meshes of the tangled net bag,

teetered on the rim while the American did a jig and a hop, midstream, then popped free and landed open on the limpid water of the Kennet and began to float serenely off to the left.

The trout was headed right.

The gentleman with the camera was reloading film at the precise moment the American had to choose between the fly box and the trout, so there is no visual record of the sudden swerve to the left, the deft netting of one fat Wheatley fly box; and since the trout had turned the bend, no one except the American saw the roll on the surface and the positive smirk as one very interesting trout rejoiced that on the other end of the line there had been such a raving maniac.

Later, the men gathered near the bridge on the main river and drank a bit more wine. Neil Patterson and another pleasant member of the club were with them now, and there was good talk and the spirited camaraderie uniquely possible along trout streams. Someone suggested that the Simpson's trout was merely one of Patterson's tethered pets, and someone else suggested that it was good the American's fly had pulled loose from the interesting trout because Bernard did not like his Kennet browns festooned like Christmas trees. The American was quietly satisfied that he would never have stooped quite so low as that.

Then John Goddard mentioned the big trout beneath the bridge and the American was invited to have a go at him. Not for me, he thought. Old Oscar—the not-to-be-caught behemoth brown. Not *that* fish—and not with *this* audience.

But the fish was high in the water, on the fin, taking the odd sedge a few feet under the bridge, and in a few moments, unable to resist, the American was tying on a Colorado King with shaky hands, squinting into the angular sun. And a few moments later he had made a truly classic puddle cast, holding the rod high and stopping the line short so that the current had three feet of slack to consume before the fly dragged.

The fly came down three inches from Old Oscar's nose. The chorus of onlookers, standing in a semicircle behind him, grew ominously silent. Old Oscar turned and floated down with the fly a few inches. The chorus audibly released breath, in a quiet whoosh.

Old Oscar took.

And the American struck, with no time to think of all the subtle minor tactics he had learned . . . and neatly snapped the fly off in the fish.

IN A FISHING HUT

In a fishing hut on the Benhams water of the River Kennet in Berkshire, I ate a sloppy cucumber sandwich, drank a mild white wine, and listened with the rest of the company gathered out of the storm as the stories began.

There was one about a lunatic who fished with bait and tied the line to his left big toe and got pulled in by a conger eel.

"I think someone is pulling our toe," said John Goddard, and he told a long, slow, very droll tale about a backcast that deftly hooked the ear of a Holstein cow, which then took off in high dudgeon across a muddy field, making the reel truly scream.

"They'll give you a great fight on light tackle," someone said.

It was warm in the fishing hut. The riverkeeper had started up a bright red fire in the cast-iron stove, I had caught my first Kennet brown that morning, and there was a profusion of food on the low center table and bottles of wine and thermos bottles of hot tea and coffee. From the open farmer's market in Newbury, Tim had bought fresh bright-yellow butter, rolls, cucumbers, a couple of different cheeses, a local pâté, and some sweet rolls—a feast. John had his usual pantry of delicacies. Hoagy and Kathy and Ross had their basket, and we were all sharing and drinking a little and bemoaning the fact that The Mayfly (important enough to be capitalized like that) had all but passed and the trout were surely glutted, and probably, anyway, it would be impossible to catch anything with such a sharp downstream wind in such a cold, pelting rain. Still, I had taken one—no matter that John had called: "What is it? A trout? Is that *really* a trout?"

When we came to the little wooden fishing hut, I had pointed out to Mari a few of The Mayfly spinners caught in spiderwebs at the edges of the windows. *Ephemera danica.* It is a big fly, only a bit smaller than our Green Drake, and often it itches and goads every fish in the river to feed on the surface. Some of the stories, which were by now mingling like the fresh pipe and cigar smoke in the tiny room, concerned the awesome spectacle of The Mayfly. Someone said he had seen eight regularly feeding fish in fixed positions in the lower end of the huge mill pool and had taken all eight of them, just like that, carefully, in order. Someone else had taken fifty-five pounds of brown trout one day during The Mayfly last year. Merely two days ago, Neil Patterson said, he could positively have *promised* me a dozen trout.

This did not trouble me overly. I have been there before. Aren't I always a couple of days late, a week early? Times too numerous to mention. And anyway, I had taken my first Kennet brown only that morning.

Someone suggested that perhaps the heavy winds would flush all the remaining spinners out of the bushes and branches. Then there might well be some real action later in the afternoon.

For a moment the little hut was lit with quiet excitement. The Mayfly might still be on! There in the little wooden hut, crammed with John and Neil and Tim and Mari and me and Hoagy and the riverkeeper and Kathy and Ross, crammed with stories and theories and past dreams and triumphs and recollections, anything seemed possible. Hope was a thing with a big white body and gossamer wings, and I noticed one or two such things over the dark cold water outside the window.

But there was some debate about what would and what would not happen, and the consensus of those who knew suggested that even *should* there be enough spinners left to interest the trout, and even *should* the wind flush them free and they should drop on the water, the downstream wind would make upstream dry-fly casting too difficult, the flies would be whisked off the water before the low-in-the-water trout could get to them, and anyway, the fish were glutted.

The logic of this position was undeniable, and I for one was inclined to accept it. Anyway, the weather outside was truly putrid and the cucumber sandwiches with fresh butter were getting better and better. I had risen steadily to five of them.

Since no one was rushing outside and everyone was dipping a bit deeper into a corner or low in a chair, and it was cozily warm and the food was good and the quiet buzz-buzz of good talk was making me feel as comfortable as Winnie the Pooh, I did not mention that, outside, there was a little snowstorm—or at least some flurries—of Mayfly spinners, sent fluttering in the wind. I raised myself a bit to watch the water and followed two of them down through the main pool. They floated merrily, a cucumber sandwich to any hungry trout, and then they disappeared—undisturbed—into the lower riffle. There was nothing, really, to make me get up. I liked the talk, which in one quarter had shifted to fly rods—and I was now listening intently to talk of tapers and relative performances.

Then Hoagy asked if I'd like to see a few fly rods he had with him and I rose to that prospect very quickly. He fetched them from his car and they proved very much worth rising to. There was an odd glass Payne that felt like a hollow stalk of dried milkweed in my hand. There was one of Hoagy's own rods, and though he had made this a bit heavy—for his own use, as he liked them—and it was too heavy for me, the rod was clearly a superb tool and made with a master craftsman's skill. Then he took out an Everett Garrison made especially for Everett Garrison. Hoagy said the old master had given it to him on the condition that it be used, not kept in a closet. Hoagy had so treated it. I said I wished I had his guts. I have four or five pieces of fine bamboo that don't regularly see water—out of fear, pure fear. Still, I'm not a collector and fishing is what rods are made for. I made a few brave resolutions, out loud, to use my own classic bamboo a bit more often—especially on water like the Kennet.

Afraid to try Hoagy's Garrison, I tried a piece of his smoked kipper instead and then made myself another sandwich. I had had six butter-and-cucumber sandwiches, two butter-and-cheese, and three butter-and-pâté; now I tried a large butter-and-butter sandwich and found it exquisitely delicious. Mari frowned. I shrugged and told her quietly that the butter was really irresistible. She muttered something wise and glum about all food's being irresistible to me. I told her this was positively my last sandwich, and anyway, could she please be wise and concerned a bit later so I could hear about the fifty—or was it eighty?—big brook trout that Hoagy and some pals were currently catching in Labrador.

Before this story was resolved, Neil was somehow in the middle of a wild, interminable trip through France, headed for the Risle with a friend who mysteriously stopped at every available bar and collected pocketfuls of sugar.

Meanwhile, John Goddard—the master of the chalkstream —was telling how, on a trip to Norway, the host had forgotten to bring the packages of food and he had to provide fish for the entire party and resorted to an old poacher's trick of sending out into the lake a dozen flies attached to a hinged instrument that . . .

"And then a monstrous dog jumped out," said Neil, "and my friend plunged his hand into his pockets . . ."

"You're pulling my toe!"

"The butter is really superb."

". . . one hundred and thirty-seven brook trout averaging . . ."

"Did the cow *really* . . ."

". . . and the dog lay down on the floor with all the sugar and licked his paws and smiled the most contented . . ."

The flurry of spinners had stopped and so had the wind. With great effort I rose to my feet and boldly suggested we try to fish again. Wasn't that a touch of sun? No, it was lightning, someone said. Didn't *anyone* want to fish? Not particularly, it seemed. I reached for a knife to cut myself a slab of straight butter, but Mari touched my hand wisely. So I went outside and in a few moments the others followed sluggishly.

Later, as I came around the bend of a carrier into a field of cows, I looked so intently at the ear of one of them that I failed to watch where I was stepping and stepped blithely into a mud sink. A lot of cows had stomped and relieved themselves there. It was quite soft and ucky. So I sank. I sank well down to my thighs and then sank a bit more down into the muck. Neil, who was guiding me, turned and said, "What the hell are you doing?" He was standing on a hard mound of grass and seemed to be walking on top of the mud. "I didn't think such things really happened to you," he said. "I thought you made them up, that they were stories. Let me take your rod."

I gave it to him, glad it was not one of my prized bamboos, and continued to tread water in the mud for another minute or two. Something in my frantic motions made the nearby cow look intently at me and give a gigantic moo. Instantly, every other cow in the large field—there may have been a hundred of them—turned, shifted position, and eyed me intently.

Neil laughed.

The cows did not.

Later, back in the hut, I became one of the stories, and I tried to drown my embarrassment in one last cucumber-and-butter sandwich, but Mari said if I didn't eat so much, maybe I would not nearly die in the mud. There was talk that the "Wilderness" section of the Kennet had been laid fallow this year because last year I had festooned the fish with so many flies and they needed time to work them out. Neil began to recount, in some happy detail, my near demise in the mud, but I interrupted him and said that I had often heard of angling writers who walked on water but none, like him, who walked on mud.

THE LAST
CHALKSTREAM IDYLL

There is a story by Morley Callaghan about a pleasant chap who took a job as an itinerant hangman because his travels led him to such interesting new places to fish. Callaghan is the huge Canadian writer who once beat up Hemingway in a Paris gym; he beat him so stoutly that the timekeeper, Scott Fitzgerald—astounded perhaps—let the round go on for several extra minutes. Hemingway never forgave either of them.

One dose of the British chalkstreams some years ago and I thought I'd lost my heart to them completely—and promptly allowed myself to become an entire subsidiary in the colonies of a British firm, with the caveat that I go to England once a year, in early June, in time for the famous mayfly hatch.

I'd hole up with the accountants and the empire builders for a week and then head off to Berkshire and the haunting Kennet River. There, hosted by Brian Clarke, John Goddard, or Neil Patterson, I'd flutter indelicately around the river, quite unlike the ghostly mayfly spinner. It was the choicest of fishing. Neil or

Brian or John would husband me along the main stem or one of the carriers, eyes peeled for a rise or a fish "on the fin." It was gorgeous water—pellucid, trouty, mined with weed. They'd spot fish I couldn't have seen with a telescope, and then I'd creep into some ghastly uncomfortable position—on my knees in high grass, perhaps—and attempt to cast to the big brown. They were good fish: better than a pound, up to three or four.

The first year I caught none; nor the second; then one year it rained and I ate cucumber sandwiches in the tiny fishing hut all day and practically did not cast. Each time the mayfly had been on the week before and *everyone* had taken fish. I shoulda been there. The weights were all carefully remembered—"one pound eight," "two pounds four," "three pounds six," "four pounds one." Then I got one, too small to have a weight, and lost one (with all my experts watching) that, on John's sharp "eye scale," went "better than four pounds two."

All that traipsing around in hip boots, waiting for a fish to show (or someone to show one to me), was less than kind and not at all comfortable. Choice as it might be, there were times when I longed for a good old egalitarian American river, where you can spend most of the day casting, not looking. And I had more than my share of disasters: losing that big fish amid the blistering silence of my audience; wading chest-deep, in my new Harris tweed jacket, into the muck, on which I thought, perhaps, I could walk. But by my fourth year I thought I knew my way around that territory.

I had two happy days on the Kennet that year. The mayfly was off but a friendly little brown sedge was on. They'd dredged the river to get rid of the heavy weed growth, and though it wasn't as pretty, there were more fish and fish happened to be taking all day. Never one for figures, I can't quote you pound and ounce on them, but I must have taken seven or eight, the largest about three pounds, and I was deliciously smug about my performance.

Toward evening on my last day, I was fishing an upper reach that had just been dredged. The water was quite deep and a bit discolored from the soft soil, so I stayed on the high bank and cast comfortably to several rising fish. The two days had been immensely satisfying and without disaster; I'd taken most of the fish I hooked and felt I'd gotten to know the river better. When we

walked down to the river from Neil's house, Neil had said that my
success was a relief to everyone. It was surely a relief to me. I'd
heard someone's wife, brought to the Kennet with some promise
of seeing the American clown perform at this annual carnival, say:
"I thought you said funny things happened when this bloke came
here. I'm terribly disappointed." Well, you can't please everyone.

I felt quite content, standing on the rim of that mud mound,
casting a little brown sedge to the circles. I looked out over the
gentle Berkshire fields, at the pinkish sky along the horizon line,
at the water as it slipped beneath an old wooden bridge, eddied,
grew riffles, and spread out into this long flat pool, and then,
suddenly, a truly large fish rose. I struck lightly, it thrashed at the
surface, and then it bore upstream heavily. It was the largest fish
I'd had on in the Kennet, better than four pounds, possibly five.
From my height, I had the advantage on it and easily walked
upstream and down, several times, to keep it above me. In ten
minutes it tired and came close to the shore and I was positive it
was a full five pounds. But how to net it? I was four or five feet
above the surface of the water, no one was around, and I had no
net with me.

I played the fish a bit more, until he turned sideways and
quiet; then I lay full length on the soft dredged sod and put the
rod on the ground beside me. I grasped the line, leaned as far over
as I dared, and came eight or ten inches short of the fish. The 6X
leader would scarcely allow me to raise it out of the water. What
to do? The evening was growing late and misty and there were ten
or twelve circles of rising fish in the pool. I wanted to catch another, perhaps two; I'd waited four years for a night like this. I
even thought of breaking the leader off, but it would have been
most ungracious to leave my fly in such a fish.

At last, not knowing how deep the water was, I decided to
climb down the bank, digging my feet into the soft mud as I went.
A lousy decision. I began to slip down the mud bank, couldn't
stop myself, and went into the water, then went on down to the
bottom of the river which was six or seven feet deep there.

I have been dunked a couple of other times in my life, once
in mud; I knew at once it could be treacherous, even fatal. So I
forced myself up against the bank, got my head above water,
screamed valiantly for help, and clawed at the mud wall. It didn't

hold. No one came. I kept slipping back, gobs of mud in my hands, on my face, my hat off and sailing downstream, the fish gone now, mud dripping down my jacket, into my shirt, filling my hip boots. For a moment or two I was quite sure I was on my way to the Great Chalkstream in the Sky. Like Everyman, I wasn't ready.

The water and mud in my hip boots made them too heavy for me to kick, the mud kept tearing away as I clawed more and more desperately into it with my hands, and I slipped back under the water twice, gurgling and choking.

The disappointed wife would have gotten her money's worth.

I've often wondered whether the crowd of them would have been too doubled over with laughter to haul me out.

In the end, I must have levitated up that mud bank, out of fear or desperation, and when I got there, I lay full face on the ground, quietly, spitting out a bit of Kennet now and then, for a full five minutes. Then I checked my rod and headed downstream to tell Neil about all the fish that were still rising.

It's more than two years since that evening. I left England the next day, disengaged myself from that firm, and have not been back.

Recently, though, I found the photocopy of a letter Neil wrote to another friend, describing the event. He probably exaggerated when he says I looked like a water buffalo, fresh from a mud bath; and I'm sure he didn't *really* laugh for ten days—and if he did, deep down he'd have been truly sad if I'd become one with the Kennet; and I doubt if my "bum print" is worth preserving on his bathroom wall, where, still plastered with mud, I must have leaned my weary rump a moment.

I didn't please the wife during that last chalkstream idyll, but Neil seems to have gained an historic monument. He shows it to everyone. Lefty Kreh—who never falls in and has been zapping those Kennet browns and regaining the honor of the colonies—told me he had been shown that spot with great reverence. It ain't that important to me: just another place where I almost got hung.

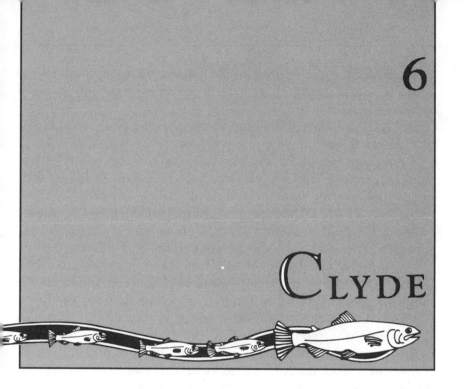

6

CLYDE

THE METAMORPHOSIS

My friend Clyde awoke one morning from uneasy dreams to find himself transformed in the night into a gigantic brown trout. It was no joke. He looked around him, hoping to see his pleasant little one-room apartment where he had lived a hermetic life since his wife cashiered him. Its walls were papered with color photographs of rising trout and natural flies the size of grouse; each corner held three or four bamboo rods in aluminum tubes; the chests of drawers were crammed with blue-dun necks and flies and fly boxes and his thirteen Princess reels; the windowsills and bookcases were packed solid with hundreds of books and catalogs and magazines devoted to the sport to which he had devoted his life. They were not there. Neither were his hands, which were fins.

Instead, he was suspended in cold moving water under an old upturned maple stump. From the clarity and size of the water, he deduced he was in Montana, or perhaps Idaho. That was fine with Clyde. If he was going to be a trout, and he had often meditated on what it would be like to be a trout (so he could tell how they thought), he'd just as well be one in Montana and Idaho.

"Well, this love of fly fishing sure takes me places I otherwise wouldn't go," he thought.

And as soon as he thought this, he realized, since he was thinking, that he had resolved an age-old problem. If he, existing under that old tree stump, could think, he could analyze his own thoughts; and since what was true for him would have to be true for all trout, he could learn what any trout thought. He was glad he had read Descartes and Kant before he went on the Halford binge.

Curiously, his esoteric studies had led him closer and closer to this point. Only the night before he had been sitting in the dimly lit room, sunk deep into his armchair in front of the lit fish-tank in which swam Oscar, his pet brown. He had been staring intently, reciting a mantra, meditating, as he did every night for four hours, when, for a moment—no, it could not be true—Oscar had (at least he thought so) told him that Foolex dubbing was the ultimate solution to the body problem. "Not quill ribbing?" he had asked audibly. "Definitely not," said Oscar. "I like you so I'll give you the straight poop: Foolex is where it's at. Anyway, tomorrow it . . . oh, you'll find out."

And so he had.

He had a thousand questions and worked his way a bit upstream, where he saw a pretty spotted tail waving gently back and forth. The trout, a hen, about three pounds, shifted slightly as Clyde nudged her and eyed him suspiciously: it was still three weeks before spawning season and she was feeling none too frisky. He opened his mouth to ask her about Foolex bodies and careened back in the current. The henfish, named Trudy, thought he was a dumb cluck and that she ought to work her way quickly past the riffle into the upper pool. Maybe this bird's clock was wrong; though she had a rotten headache, he might even attack her.

Clyde, ever watchful, immediately deduced from her defensiveness that communication among trout, like communication between fly fishermen and bocce players, was impossible. He'd have to answer his questions by himself. This is never easy, particularly not on an empty stomach. He had not eaten anything since the pepperoni sandwich fifteen hours earlier; and he was not dumb enough to think he could soon get another, since the Belle Deli was two thousand miles away.

There was a silver flash and Clyde turned and shot up after it, turning on it as it slowed and turned and lifted up in the current. But he was too late. A little twelve-inch rainbow had sped from behind a large rock and grasped the thing, and it was now struggling with ludicrous futility across stream, the silver object stuck in its lower jaw.

"Incredible!" Clyde thought. "How could I have been so dumb?" He had not seen the hooks; he had not distinguished between metal and true scales. If he who had studied Halford, Skues, Marinaro, and Schwiebert could not distinguish a C. P. Swing from a dace tartare, what hope had any of his speckled kin? He shivered with fear as he asked himself: "Are *all* trout this dumb?"

He worked his way back under the upturned stump, into the eddy, and sulked. This was a grim business. He noticed he was trembling with acute anxiety neurosis but could not yet accept that *all* trout were neurotic. He was positively starved now and would have risen to spinach, which he hated.

Bits and pieces of debris, empty nymph shucks, a couple of grubs swept into the eddy. He nosed them, bumped them, took them into his mouth, spit some of them out. By noon he had managed to nudge loose one half-dead stone-fly nymph, *Pteronarcys californica;* he had nabbed one measly earthworm; and he had found a few cased caddises. Most food, he noted, came off the bottom; that's where it was at. The lure had come down from the surface; he should have known. He was learning something new every minute.

By now he had recognized that he was in the Big Hole River, below Divide; he was sure he had once fished the pool. Settled into that eddy under the stump, he now knew why he had not raised a fish here: the current swung the food down below the undercut bank, but his flies had been too high up in the water. The way to fish this run was almost directly downstream from his present position, casting parallel to the bank so the nymph would have a chance to ride low and slip down into the eddy.

He was trying to plot the physics of the thing, from below, and was getting dizzy, when he realized he could starve flat down to death if he didn't stop trying to be a trout fisherman and settle for being a trout. His stomach felt pinched and dry; his jaws ached to clamp down on a fresh stone-fly nymph or, yes, a grasshopper. That's what he wanted. He suddenly had a mad letch for grasshoppers—and there was absolutely nothing he could do to get one. He was totally dependent upon chance. "A trout's lot," he thought, "is not a happy one."

Just then the surface rippled a bit, perhaps from a breeze, and a couple of yards upstream, he saw the telltale yellow body, kicking legs, and molded head of a grasshopper. It was August, and he knew the grasshoppers grew large around the Big Hole at that time of the year. It came at him quickly, he rose sharply to it, then stopped and turned away with a smirk. "Not me. Uh-uh. A Dave's Hopper if I ever saw one. Not for this guy." And as he thought this, Trudy swept downstream past him, too quick for him to warn, and nabbed the thing in an abrupt little splash. Then she turned, swam up by him, seemed to shake her head and say, "How dumb a cluck can you be?"

So it *had* been the real thing. Nature was imitating art now. Oh, he could taste the succulent hopper.

Another splatted down, juicy and alive, and he rose again, paused, and it shot downstream in a rush. He'd never know about that one.

Oh, the existential torment of it! "And I thought deciding which artificial fly to use was hard!"

Two more hoppers, then a third splatted down. He passed up one, lost a fin-race with Trudy for the third. She was becoming a pill.

He could bear it no longer. He'd even eat a Nick's Crazylegs if it came down. Anything. Anything to be done with the torment, the veil of unknowing, the inscrutability, which was worse than the pain in his gut, as it always is.

And then he saw it.

It was a huge, preposterous, feathered thing with a big

black hook curled up under it. Some joker with three thumbs had thought it looked like a grasshopper. The body was made of Foolex. How could Oscar possibly have thought that body anything other than insulting? Clyde's hook jaw turned up in a wry smile; he wiggled his adipose fin. The fly came down over him and he watched it safely from his eddy. And it came down again. Then again. Twelve. Thirteen times. Trudy had moved twice in its direction. He could tell she was getting fairly neurotic about it.

Foolex? That body could not fool an imbecile. It *was* an insult!

Eighteen. Twenty times the monstrosity came over him. He was fuming now. How *dare* someone throw something like that at him! Had they no respect whatsoever? If that's all fishermen thought of him, what did it matter. He was bored and hungry and suffering from a severe case of *angst* and humiliation. Nothing mattered. It was a trout's life.

He rose quickly and surely now, turning as the thing swept down past him on the thirty-third cast. He saw it hang in the surface eddy for a moment. He opened his mouth. Foolex? It infuriated him! It was the ultimate insult.

He lunged forward. And at the precise moment he knew exactly what trout see and why they strike, he stopped being a trout.

SALMO PSYCHOSIS

There came a time in my friend Clyde's life when the pressures of his addiction became more than a reasonable man could bear. So he sought professional help. He went to a doctor. The doctor specialized in diseases of the brain and nervous system afflicted by too much dwelling upon the trout. After one short session, the doctor found where Clyde's symptoms pointed inescapably: "Ya," he told me. "He's vun of dem. Dis Clyde all right ist eine trouptf nut."

The affliction is neither as new nor as rare as some people

think. Some of those people who think it is rare are publishers, eighty-seven of whom rejected Dr. Helmut von Rainbogen's two-thousand-page-book, *Salmo Psychosis: The Hidden Enemy.* Von Rainbogen's book catalogued 12,654,837 bona fide cases of *Salmo* psychosis, dating from the fourth century B.C. The publishers, though, said there was no market for the book, particularly because it had no sex scenes; they also thought there was too much emphasis on western *Salmo* psychosis, and that, in their view, from Madison Avenue, no one bought books west of the Mississippi unless they were about Zen or est or the lettuce boycott.

"Vhat vee have here," von Rainbogen told me in the waiting room when he came out with his arm around Clyde's shoulder, "ist eine truly classic case. Clyde Pfisht ist eine absolutely classic troupft nut." I tried to place his accent. It sounded like an Austro-Prussian-Croatian dialect by way of left field. He smiled benignly at Clyde, pretended to fly cast an imaginary rod toward an imaginary river at the other end of his waiting room, and said, condescendingly, I thought, "Ya, ya, Herr Pfisht. Dot's vhat's on your mind, no?"

"Yeah, I'd rather be out pfishting than fritzing around with a loon like you," said Clyde, and I was again won over by my friend's candor.

While Dr. Rainbogen stroked his goatee and nodded vigorously, I scanned the waiting room. There were three aquarium tanks, filled with piranhas. On the walls were blown-up photographs of men and women shredded by sharks. Above the couch, there was a framed news clipping from Alaska describing an attack by killer rainbow trout on three Eskimo kids. Worse, in a plastic case there was a plastic eye into which was stuck the hook point of a Quill Gordon. But most shocking, when I looked closely, were the mottled backs of the piranhas and the bright red dots on the sharks: they were trout in savage bodies.

"It is dangerous, this pfly pfishting for the troupfts, no?" said the doctor.

I cannot repeat what Clyde said.

A week later I brought my friend back. He'd had a miserable week though I had done what I could to comfort him. I told him he'd enjoy his fly fishing more if he could keep it in proportion. I told him that the season was only a few months off—"Seventy-three days," he said—and he'd enjoy it much more this year.

"Don't be an idiot," he told me. "If this lunatic has his way, I'll never fish again. He's a deprogrammer—the kind they use for runaway kids. If he cures me, I'll have absolutely nothing to live for. I'm sane. I'm perfectly sane. I'm as sane as anyone."

Clyde did not in fact have all his marbles. He sometimes thought he was a trout. He divided the world into fly fishers and lunatics. He became manic during the hatch periods and depressive out of season. He had paranoid fits that his children wanted to roast marshmallows with his Payne rods. He accused the IRS of spoiling Opening Day for him each year. He haunted New York's garment district like a hog after truffles, searching for scrap pieces of fur to put into his dubbing blender. One or two of these and similar qualities you will find in your average basic fly fisher; together, as von Rainbogen has written, they're absolute evidence of *Salmo* psychosis.

After four long sessions, the doctor took me aside and said: "He vill not let go. He is holding tight to der primal gonnegtions." He looked at me intently and said: "He really likes this pfly pfishting, no?"

"Maybe," I said. "Have you tried it?"

"Never, never," he said. "You do dis ding?"

I admitted that I had been known to do it.

"It is pfun, maybe?"

"Yeah, it's pfun."

"Hmmmm," said the doctor, stroking his goatee. "Der ist eine fine line, maybe, between genius and madness, no?"

Later that spring I was about to end a quiet early-May afternoon on the Beaverkill and was sitting on a rock smoking my pipe. It had been a pleasant, unhurried time—all I could want of a day's fishing. Some Hendricksons had shown about one o'clock, but no fish came to them. Then, about four, there was some deliberate feeding to the spinners. There were buds of green peppering the hillside and light waves of warmth in the air, and in the end I had taken four difficult trout on gossamer leader tippets. A pleasant spring day. Some difficult fishing. Some good stalking and casting. No disasters. A measure of success. Quite enough for me, thank you.

Through the trees, I suddenly saw two figures approaching from Schoolhouse Pool. Something about the way they walked and the loud sounds one of them made forced me to watch them. In a few moments they were near and I knew them.

One man was a walking Orvis catalog. His vest was crammed to overflowing, he carried two rods, a huge wooden net flapped behind him, and a smaller one was tucked into the belt of his waders. The mandatory fleece hatband was filled with fifty or sixty flies. He was gesticulating wildly, spreading his arms to show the size of something that he had perhaps lost or caught. And his voice was high-pitched, nearly insane, in a key I only hear along the Madison River when the salmon-fry hatch is on.

The man was clean shaven and that three-dollar accent was gone, but it was surely Dr. Helmut von Rainbogen.

Clyde, usually the most talkative of companions astream, was stone silent.

"Big Hole . . . steelhead . . . Alaska . . . Muddler . . . no-hackle . . . thorax tie . . . up-eye . . . riffling hitch . . . pupae . . . 6X . . . sipping rise . . . Tricos . . . reach cast . . . flop cast . . ."

The words must have swarmed up out of the doctor's unconscious. I tried to think of how many troupft nuts he had disengaged from words like this. Now the words came back, all of them, and he was shouting them madly into Clyde's ear. He was one with the Great Collective Trout Unconscious.

"Elk Hair Caddis . . . masking hatch . . . spinner fall . . . halfhitch . . . no kill . . . Battenkill . . . nail knot . . . paradun . . . Rogue . . . spring creek . . . multiple hatch . . . saddle hackle . . ."

I knew the words but I could make no sense—if there was any—of how they were put together. The man sounded berserk.

I scrunched down in the bushes to let them pass.

As they did, I heard Clyde say: "But I'm bushed, Doc. Worn out. We've fished twenty-seven days in a row, twelve hours a day. I have a job. I have kids. I think I once had a wife."

Clyde, normally one of the swiftest men along a streambank,

was falling behind. He did not hear something the quick doctor had said.

"What? No! No, I don't want to!" he shouted. "I know. I know I'm getting a fat fee..."

The doctor was around the bend now.

Clyde shouted: "But the book, Doc. Don't you think we ought to work on the book? No. We've done enough research. Doc! *Trout and Salvation* will be a best-sell—"

And then they were both around the bend.

FAME AND FORTUNE

THE COMPLETE BOOK OF FLY FISHING FOR TROUT

Introduction

I once swore I would never write a *complete* practical book. It's boastful and I'm not all that practical. I also once swore off cigars and hard likker. Anyway, I need the money and the fame won't hurt.

If you want to thank someone for the brevity of this book, thank my wife, who loathes fishing. Without her, I'd have written an epic.

Chapter 1: The Trout

Trout recommend themselves to fly fishermen because they eat flies. That they do not always eat flies, especially fake flies—and who can blame them?—is another good recommendation. Trout live in rivers and lakes, each different from the other. This different-ness and the differentness of anglers, and the different tackle they manage to use, and the differentness of each trout, and other strange differentnesses too numerous to mention, makes fishing for trout wondrously different from eel fishing in the Hudson River. There is a well-known maxim in Aristotle's "Historia Animalium": If you've caught one eel, man, you've caught them all.

I once knew a man who talked to trout, but he found that they never talked back.

Chapter 2: Gear

In previous incarnations, trout fishermen were itinerant junk dealers who roamed from town to town with all their purchases and wares on their backs and hanging around their necks. I deduced this one day on the Beaverkill by looking closely at a fine specimen of the species and laughing so hard that, for some unaccountable reason, he threw a De-Liar at me. For most fly fishermen, more is better. As I grow older, less is best.

As a result, I no longer take with me along the streams: telescopes, binoculars, walkie-talkies, hand warmers, umbrellas, fly-tying equipment, extra rods, a two-week supply of Fig Newtons, ostrich eggs, extra waders, the last three selections from the Field & Stream Book Club, children under the age of thirty, or a portable television set.

Though the principle of simplicity is logical and well founded, I do not advise eliminating rod, reel, line, and flies.

Chapter 3: Basic Techniques

You cannot cast a fly until you have set up your equipment properly. This may seem too obvious to mention, unless you have tried to cast with your line strung through the keeper ring. I do not recommend this. Otherwise, follow your natural impulses. Only don't follow them too far.

Chapter 4: Stream Lore

The river is nothing like the city. It has its own laws and you must learn some of them before you will catch any trout on a fly. Bless it for not being like the city!

Chapter 5: Hatches

"A little learning is a dangerous thing," says Alexander Pope. "Drink deep, or taste not the Pierian spring."

On the other hand, Pope knew Latin, did not realize that there are thousands of bugs in American trout streams, and had not the faintest idea that a person drinking too deeply in entomology could go loony.

Pope also said: "True wit is Nature to advantage dressed"—another extremely valuable maxim for fly fishermen. Paraphrased, this means: Never go to a trout stream without a good supply of wit along, especially if it's dressed by Poul Jorgensen.

Hatch matching is a rapidly evolving art. Today we have no-hackle flies and no-wing spinners; tomorrow, the Emperor's New Fly.

Chapter 6: No-Hatches

When no flies are visibly hatching, you can quite safely assume—assuming your eyesight is adequate and if not you should have your eyes examined twice a year—that no flies are visibly hatching. "Heard melodies are sweet," says John Keats, "but those unheard are sweeter still." (That has no relevance, except that Keats once knew a girl whose father knew a man who was reputed once to have caught a trout; anyway, Keats developed the concept of "negative capability," which is a valuable capability for fly fishermen to develop.)

A trout cannot eat what he doesn't see, or what is not there; but he also cannot go to the 21 Club, though I'll bet he'd like to. If you can't figure out where the trout are, or what they're taking, try the nearest bar.

Chapter 7: Sunshine and Shade

Hamlet's statement "I am too much i' th' sun" is relevant here. None of us like to be examined too closely, especially if we have hives. Trout don't get hives but they're pathologically shy, wallflowers of an underwater sort. Frankly, they're pretty shady characters and very antisocial.

Chapter 8: Drag

If you saw a piece of steak moving unnaturally on your plate, would you eat it?

Chapter 9: Fly Tying

This is a very cunning activity, but I do not recommend your taking it up if you know Ted Niemeyer, Poul Jorgensen, Art Flick, Rene Harrop, Edson Leonard, Dave Whitlock, Harry Darbee, Walt Dettee, Dick Talleur, Del Bedinotti, Helen Shaw, Dan Blanton, or some other individual with thirteen fingers and a good supply of blue dun hackles who remembers you generously at Christmas.

Chapter 10: Playing and Netting Fish

If I have ever engaged in such activities, I've forgotten.

Chapter 11: Travel

I once knew a guy who spent five thousand dollars traveling to Scotland and staying at posh resorts on three of the best rivers in the country. He fished every day from daybreak until after dusk, until his arms were lead and he was willing to take up sleep as a sport. He did not catch a fish.

I don't catch any on West Eighty-fourth Street, either.

Chapter 12: The Literature of Angling

A couple of billion too many words have been written about fly fishing. I have contributed to this mess. Why are so many words written? Perhaps because they are read. Why are they read? Perhaps because fly fishermen fish too little. To pursue the argument further, we can stop all this damned pollution by fishing more, which I recommend.

Probably none of it will make you a better fly fisherman, anyway—and any novel by Hardy, Melville, Waugh, Dickens, Tolstoy, Dostoyevski, Sterne, Proust, Joyce, Hemingway, Marquez, Faulkner, or Jane Austen is better worth your time. These will make you a wiser human being, which has a good chance of making you a wiser fly fisherman. But don't count on it.

Fly fishing has a long history. It is very long.

Epilogue

Many years ago I learned two lessons: If you destroy a trout river, it will not be there; if you kill a trout, it will no longer be in the river.

There is a corollary worth noting: If there are no rivers and no trout, there can be no fly fishing for trout.

And then I won't be able to make my fortune by writing *Son of the Complete Book of Fly Fishing for Trout.*

ADVENTURES IN THE FUR TRADE

Walking to and from my old office, I had to pass every day through New York City's fur district. This is an area roughly between Sixth and Seventh avenues and Twenty-seventh through Thirtieth streets; at least a lot of it is there, and some buildings—first through thirtieth floors—are wall-to-wall fur cutters, fur merchants, fur storage firms, fur designers, and fur wholesalers. The significance of this concentrated marketplace eluded me for more than four years.

But not even I can be that dumb that long.

One day last winter I passed a huge dump-bin in the middle of West Twenty-eighth Street; it was swarming with dump-bin scavengers. Thirty or forty people, men and women, were tearing at cardboard boxes filled with mink scraps. They were silent but intent about their business, and they were quite particular: they chose only the larger scraps, a foot or more in length. The rest of the stuff—slim cuttings of irregular size and shape—they simply threw back into the dump-bin or onto the street. In all, there must have been a ton of mink, mostly the smaller scraps that nobody wanted. It was everywhere.

I had been tying some small caddis flies and vaguely remembered a British friend who used mink for his wing material. So, nonchalantly, aloof from the serious picking, I picked up a few small cuttings, enough to tie a couple of dozen mink-wing caddis flies. Then I shook my head sadly at the hive of disreputable scavengers and headed home.

But in the night, while it poured, I dreamed of mink. I saw the dump-bin and the horde of silent vultures; but mostly I saw the scraps of mink that no one else had any use for. I woke early the next morning, forgot to shave, and rushed downtown an hour early, full of great expectations. I'd collect up a barrel of the stuff; I'd trade it for other materials; I'd swap it for flies; I'd sell it; I'd corner the mink market; I'd be rich; I'd retire to Montana.

But the dump-bin was gone and the efficient New York street-cleaning machines had left only a few scraps, which I picked out of the wet streets and stuffed surreptitiously into my pockets.

When you are unaware of a thing, you do not see it. I fished for years during leaf-roller "falls" before I saw them. And when I finally noticed those delicate green worms, I wondered how I had missed them for so long. They were everywhere: on the branches, on the leaves, dropping down to the surface of the water on spidery threads, on my rod, on my neck, on my vest, in my waders. How could I *not* have seen them?

I dreamed of mink and searched every morning for mink— and thus began my strange adventures in the fur trade.

Early and late I hunted fur.

One day I found a truck hauling out rabbits' feet—millions of them—and plucked a dozen out of the garbage and wedged them into my always crowded pockets. One night I found a small quantity of some exceptionally soft chinchilla cuttings, packed them up carefully, and sent them to Craig Mathews, the superb West Yellowstone tier. He tied me up a couple of mini-streamers that were bound to be lethal, and from then on I could not keep my nose out of the gutter. I'd shuffle down Twenty-eighth Street, tipping up garbage-pail tops, poking into green bags, walking off the curb and into alleyways. I found beaver cuttings, some mink, a bit of sable now and then, a couple of fox half-tails, some Australian opossum. One night I almost got hit by a truck backing up in the dark, and I must surely have been taken for one of New York's lunatic street people. Frankly, I didn't notice. And if I had, I wouldn't have cared.

I'd heard about road kills and the fine pelts that could be found on highways—from Eric Leiser's versatile groundhog to deer. But this was ridiculous. There was gold in the streets, just for the picking, and it was clean.

Off the stuff went to Craig and back came some of the most beautiful little mink caddis, #22, you've ever seen—and an enthusiastic letter saying that he'd take all I could find. We called the flies—in case you care—the Lyons-Mathews Seventh Avenue Specials. Not only my fortune but also my fame was assured.

My family, my business associates, and anyone else who saw me with all those fur scraps tumbling out of my pockets surely thought me mad. I was in ecstasy. I neglected my business and my friends; I ate lunch while walking and searching; I did not think trout, I thought chinchilla.

And then the flow stopped. For two weeks in January and early February, with snow and slush spoiling the streets, I found no more than a piece of rug and a hank of lamb's wool. Was the cutting season over? Should I go directly to the dealers? Somewhere out there, in the labyrinth of the fur district, was a fortune. Scrap fur, which must exist by the carload, which was being thrown out somewhere, by someone down there, every day, must have a yearly street value, if converted into flies, of at least twenty-four million dollars.

I couldn't leave my business during the prime hours of the morning and afternoon, much as I longed to do so, so I enlisted the aid of my good friend Justin. Ah, Justin! Never was there a more passionate fly fisherman or friend. On a perfectly grizzly March afternoon, he called me from a pay phone in the street and said he'd found the mother lode. Our fortunes were made. The phone connection was poor so I told him to rush over and we'd huddle on it.

Minutes later he was there, wet as a Labrador retriever. I dropped a mess of insignificant contracts and manuscripts in a heap on the floor and he gave me the dope: there was a scrap-fur broker, in fact a couple of them. He had been to a dozen cutters and dealers, and they all said they sold their scraps by the pound to a broker. Justin had found him, in a ground-floor, cement-floored room, surrounded by mountains of fur. "You never saw so much, Nick," he said, his voice rising. "There are bales of it, hundreds of them, up to the ceiling, all over."

So I raced out. It was three P.M., a Tuesday. Justin was right. Nutria, Polish nutria, mink, ermine, beaver, sable, chinchilla, five kinds of fox, Australian opossum—butt ends, tails, body fur, thin cuttings, fat cuttings, head pieces, belly slabs: you would not believe the amounts. It was a fly tier's Valhalla. And it was all dirt cheap. The broker filled a three-foot-high paper bag with Australian opossum and said, "Give me three bucks, make it two—you look like a nice guy." And Justin and I took all we could carry, enough to make fifty million flies, and hauled it all, struggling, both arms full, up the wet streets to my office. We were too excited—or exhausted—to talk.

Then I spent a couple of hours packing it up in cardboard crates and shipping it west, in trade for flies. In all, by the time the trout season opened, I'd spent dozens of hours hauling, packing, and shipping box after box of that stuff to tiers; and bits and pieces of it stuck to my clothes, spread out over the floor of my office, would not be extricated from the rug, nearly lost me an employee who shrieked when she saw a fox head in my pocket, and very nearly drove my little business into bankruptcy. Worse, we glutted the market and turned my little gold mine into a pig's ear. And I grew bored by it—oh, how bored I was by April after all the lugging and packing, with nutria coming out of my ears, after shipping all those dozens of cartons of fur cuttings. Justin was, too.

I might have continued my madness for months longer but the fates were with me: our lease was up and we had to move. Fortunately, we moved to the paper and printing district, where I have yet to find a use for the cardboard crates and boxes of paper scraps I pass every day.

It is months now and sometimes I get an itch to get my hand

back into the fur trade. Now and again I'll get off the subway a few stations early, in my old stomping grounds, to check a few of my favorite haunts. They're still there: the garbage pails two doors from the corner of Seventh Avenue and Twenty-eighth Street where I found all the sable; the rutted corner of Seventh and Twenty-seventh, where I could *always* get a pocketful of chinchilla in the morning; the alleyway up Twenty-seventh where they dump the rabbits' feet. I still pick up a few choice scraps when I go, for old times' sake, but my heart isn't in it anymore. It's May, and I'm working a bit harder and longer, so I can take off the odd Friday and head for the mountains. I happen to prefer fish to fur.

But the gold's there, and Justin and I will tell you where it is—if you promise not to get us involved in the fur trade again.

MY SALMON BOOK

In the long year and a half since my first (and last) salmon trip, I have suffered periodically from *Salmo* psychosis—salmon on the brain, of the *salar* variety. I kept seeing the silvered turn of that cockfish near the boulder at the tail end of the Strengir section of the Grimsa. I kept thinking of which fish I took and why. I kept remembering the spurts of water, the "ticks," when salmon nosed the fly or struck short at the tooled lip above the great falls. And for a great while I tied salmon flies almost every night and read deeply in Kelson, Hardy, Hunt, and Wulff.

Last winter Pierre visited me for more than a month, and when Pierre is present so, always, are thoughts of salmon. He is a notorious fisher for the salmon. He has fished for them, from his teens, in Iceland and Scotland and Canada and France. He has been a salmon guide and a fighter for salmon.

No one I know more embodies the fly fisherman's total devotion to his sport than Pierre Affre. He is an absolute fount of information. He has fished from Africa to the arctic with the long rod, and he holds more than a dozen European casting records. The great French tournament caster Pierre Creusevaut taught him when Pierre was in his midteens and he won the junior French championship soon afterward. He took three medals in world casting championships, was European champion in salmon distance, and eight times held the French fly-casting championship. Pierre is not a large man—perhaps five feet six inches, 135 pounds—but you can see as he moves that he has great athletic prowess. There is a kind of catlike, stalking quality to his every movement. And he takes his fishing so seriously that, when he came to stay with me last winter, he was in a terrible funk. It wasn't a midlife crisis because Pierre is only thirty—but he was not a happy man.

The problem was this: he's a veterinarian and five years ago a Paris vet's salary was inflated—so Pierre had only to work a mere few months of the year to be able to fish the rest: more than three hundred days of fly fishing most years. Some of us had called him Lucky Pierre. But inflation was changing everything. Travel was vastly more expensive, and a veterinarian's wages had not kept pace with the rise in all else. Pierre had in fact been forced to give up his Left Bank apartment on rue Guenegard, several blocks from the Seine, and had been living here and there, his mountains of tackle stacked in backpacks ready for the next trip. His rent money was needed for travel. But even that was not a solution. At thirty, poor Pierre was terrified—or so he seemed to me—that he would have to fish less than ten months of the year.

Though this is not precisely my problem, and I sometimes have some small difficulty sympathizing with my friend Pierre, I tried to be a generous soul when, with tremors in his voice, he first called from Paris to explain his plan. He would study at the Animal Medical Center in New York City for several months, learn surgery (which paid more per hour), and thus he would again be able to work less each year.

It was a canny fly fisherman's solution to one of life's little problems.

But the plan did not work.

Soon after he arrived, Pierre fell in with some low types at the Theodore Gordon Flyfishers, was induced to give a slide show or two, and at my insistence began to instruct me in the arts of salmon fishing. Worse would come later.

He bought several two-handed salmon rods, which he loved, and at Riverside Park showed me how to use them. He said he preferred the big rods so he could fight the salmon, not let them fight him. Then he permanently spread out all manner of flosses and feathers and squirrel tails on my dining-room table and taught me to tie salmon flies. The way Pierre tied them they were simpler to make than trout flies, and I started to tie with a vengeance. I really wasn't too bad at it, either.

In fact, I was learning so much and dreaming so much about salmon that I began to think I had found that thing I was born to do: write a book on salmon fishing.

The world did not precisely need a new book by me on salmon fishing, but one must do what one must do.

The problem was: I didn't know much about salmon fishing.

Well, that hadn't bothered 16,823 other guys who wrote books on some aspect of fly fishing last year. And I had, after all, a full week of experience; perhaps I only needed some research.

I read with great intensity and care the gorgeous new reprint of *The Salmon Fly* by Colonel George M. Kelson. It is quite a remarkable book, handsomely redone by the Anglers and Shooters Press, and it was clearly the work of someone who knew whereof he spoke. Colonel Kelson had in fact said that one could not authoritatively speak about salmon fishing until he had caught three thousand salmon—which he had done. I had caught 2,988 fewer than that, or thereabouts—I don't count well. But I had *Salmo* psychosis and I began to think that I could know everything important about salmon fishing if I stood on Colonel Kelson's broad shoulders and got Pierre to help me.

How much was there to know?

After my first hour of salmon fishing, when I had not caught a fish, I was quite sure that I could not possibly learn how to do this new thing. There was no logic to it: I could not see the fish (at least not where I began), they were not feeding nor would they ever feed, I had thirty-seven different fly patterns from which to choose and no wherewithal with which to make a choice. I was not even sure there were salmon in a particular lie I was fishing (which gave me waves of a slightly lunatic feeling).

But after a mere week of intense fishing, I learned a few rules. Bigger flies worked better in bigger water. Bright flies worked best during bright times of the day and dark during dark. Some of the simplest flies, with squirrel-tail wings, worked far better than the more elaborate, far prettier patterns. When a fish came, you counted to thirty and went after it again, sometimes with a smaller fly, sometimes with one a little larger (to increase what Schwiebert called the "irritation factor").

I learned to vibrate the rod tip a little in certain water and to use a Crossfield retrieve when there was not enough current to swing the fly. I learned to use the riffling hitch and how to be very very patient when, cast after cast, nothing happened. I learned to work my way downstream a half step at a time. And when Pierre showed me how to tie a decent Blue Charm, Hairy Mary, Green Butt, White Wing, and a no-name all-black fly that he said was his favorite, I thought I would take the mystery out of salmon fishing once and for all and do my salmon book.

I kept writing my one page of salmon facts over and over and over and finally realized that I chiefly needed to pick Pierre's brain. That was all. And I was on the verge of picking it or plagiarizing it or whatever the 16,823 other guys who know nothing about their subject do, when Pierre suddenly noticed that it was March and he announced that he had to start serious training for the tarpon season in Homosassa Springs, Florida. Tarpon? I'd thought he was a salmon addict.

Pierre began by running six or seven miles a day. That should have told me something about his state of mind. I had hoped to listen dutifully, with pen in hand, to Pierre lecture on the salmon, but with March came a torrent of tarpon madness.

"They're only overgrown herring," I told him.

"You must see them, Neek," he said, "when they are, how-you-say, daisy-chaining and a two-hundred-pounder breaks from the chain for your fly."

I remembered that our mutual friend Charles Ritz, when well into his eighties, had told me one day at lunch that saltwater fly fishing (which he had just tried for the first time) was "for men with hard stomachs: it's like sex" (which he had not just tried for the first time) "after lunch."

But I told Pierre that, as usual, I would probably be too busy to fish for tarpon with him, and anyway, I wanted him to tell me about salmon. I had salmon on the brain, not big herring.

"You cannot miss them," he said. "They are fantastic. That is not possible you should be too busy. *Impossible!"*

And he went on and on, infectiously, and I never did get his mind away from big herring and back to the noble salmon. In April he went back to Paris and worked for a week or so, maybe eleven days—and then in May he went to Homosassa, hooked and lost several world-record tarpon, appeared again briefly on West Eighty-fourth Street, and then took off for somewhere and then went to Gabon and was last heard from in the Amazon, a few weeks ago . . .

So my salmon book languishes and I rather think the world can do without it, or should wait for Pierre to slow down enough to write one of his own.

But the new season is starting and Craig Woods has been after me to do a little serious chub fishing, and we're thinking that perhaps what the world really needs from a couple of serious chub-slayers, what it has been waiting patiently for, is a book called *The Masters on the Chub.*

THE MASTERS
ON THE CHUB

Mr. Craig Woods and I have long recognized the gigantic closet audience for a classic and truly authoritative book on the chub. It is a much-maligned gamefish, often caught and vividly remembered, but rarely with sufficient affection. We had thought to call it *Challenge of the Chub* but in the end were persuaded that the word "chub" already connotes challenge; anyway, we realized that no one or two sane men could do the broad subject justice, so we wanted a title that would reflect the efforts of many acknowledged experts, of whom there are more than any of us care to admit. We have divided the final book into twelve brilliant chapters, each written by a "master on the chub." Unfortunately, we have not been able to find a publisher for this important book, so I am taking the liberty of sending out this synopsis as a teaser, with the hopes that some fishing-book editor with vision will recognize that the chub may be

the fish of the future and publish the wretched thing so we can begin
our path-breaking book called *Tricos for Gar.*

1
"Mystique of the Chub" by Speecum Swill

A concise ninety-four-page history of the lure and lore of chub
fishing on four continents, with special attention to Charlemagne's
three-week flirtation with chub fishing, the refinement of chubbing
techniques by Halford, the effect of polypropylene on the sensibility
of the chub-fly tier, a detailed look at forty-six little-known chubbing clubs and the wines they served with fried, baked, broiled,
smoked, sautéed, marinated, and raw chub, along with recipes for
"Chub Wellington," "Chub Fondue," and "Chubby Chub." Swill
notes, with more than a pinch of irony, that McClane quotes
Thoreau as saying the chub tastes "like brown paper salted."

2
"Biology of the Chub" by Seymour Veynes

A dense, almost unreadable chapter on *Semotilus corporalis*, which
makes important distinctions (in thirty-seven forgettable pages)
between the true American chub, or fallfish; and *Leuciscus
leuciscus*, the dace; and *Squalius cephalus*, a European cyprinid.
There are detailed schematic drawings of the anatomy of the
chub, feeding charts, and an almost pornographic description of
the chub's sex life with enlightening comments on spring spawning, which figures importantly in Chapter 10.

3
"Finer Tackle for Bigger Chub—The 5–8 Club" by Haight
X. Leedor

All is relative. A five-inch chub on an 8X leader and a half-ounce
Dickerson rod can seem like a five-inch chub on an 8X leader and
a half-ounce Dickerson rod.

4
"Fishing the Dry Fly for Chub on Rivers and Streams and Everywhere Else" by Fyne Aire
*

We are especially proud of this chapter. It is an edited version of Dr. Aire's 937-page doctoral dissertation for the Women's Studies Department at South Delaware Community College. With no effort at all we have compacted the essence of his remarkable treatise into two pungent pages.

5
"How to Kill the Chub of Your Life on Supernymphs" by Lord Humphrey Crud

Our British contribution, by a peer who devoted his life to the pursuit of a better chub nymph and then, when he found it, killed himself with an 8/0 O'Shaughnessy hook.

6
"How to Use the Shooting-Taper Line for Chub—and Suckers!" by Moe Longer and Mae B. Longer

This famous brother and sister team have cornered the shooting-taper corner of the fly-fishing-for-chub world and they are welcome to it. Their description of a chub's fight at the end of a 134-foot cast, in fast water, is interminable.

7
"Fishing for Chub When There Is No Sewer Discharge" by Dr. R. U. Kidding

Chub *can* be caught out of the effluent line! This is proved conclusively by Dr. Kidding, who adapted the gas mask for Discharge Chubbing, then nobly pioneered a sport bound to bankrupt him.

8
"The Silver Chub in Fast Water" by G.R.E.A.T. DeBrunch

This chapter introduces the revolutionary concept of the induced or "hokey" hatch, created by nine ambidextrous casters, each with a rod in each hand, simultaneously casting Iwamasa Chubbing Duns into fast water at midnight to simulate a hatch of *Ephemerella canadensis*. DeBrunch is credited with the maxim: "I never met a chub I could not induce."

9
"What the Chub Said" by R. E. Corder

Not a thing.

10
"Fierce and Unusual Methods of Catching and Killing Chub"

The author of this startling chapter is loath to reveal himself at this time since he fears some backlash from the millions of devoted chubbers across the country, some of whom have already indicated that they think the author is really a *Salmo* man in *Semotilus* garb, attempting to undermine the Chub Party by eliminating the chub. He is currently being investigated by the A.S.P.C.C., the Association for the Prevention of Cruelty to Chubs, whose Director of Moral Conscience is Mari Highhorse Lyons; in her recent *People* magazine interview on the Chub Question, this auspicious woman quoted Coleridge, "He prayeth best who loveth best all things both great and small," and went on to say, "I don't like to see prejudice rear any of its ugly heads." We feel strongly that the author of this chapter has been sorely maligned. Though he does not advocate barbless hooks, fine leaders, or catch-and-release, he is foursquare behind the chub. In addition, we support the concept that all forms of chubbing, short of dynamite and poison, are honorable.

11
"Future of the Chub" by Willy Makemore

The introduction of the controversial Makemore-Vibert Box,

marketed under the slogan "Chub Galore for Rich and Poor," assures an all-too-bright future for the chub.

12
"The Royal Order of the Chub" by I. M. Looney

The president of the one remaining chub club in the world, now reduced to a single member, himself, gives a revealing and dramatic behind-the-scenes portrait of the heyday of the Royal Order—including the famous confrontation between Hy Lee Dryford and Ollie Wetsworth, in which the former proclaimed, "You *cannot* fish the subsurface fly for chub," and the latter replied, "You bet your sweet Cahill I can—and *have.*" Now 107 and unable to resign because he took out a life membership in 1911, the Honorable I. M. Looney charts the decline and fall of the once-great club after the Dryford-Wetsworth Controversy. Particularly moving is the account of how the Vice President, Membership Secretary, and Treasurer defected four years ago to Dace Unlimited. The Royal Order of the Chub meets every day except when Mr. Looney is in shock therapy.

Librarians will be interested in knowing that our book includes a definitive bibliography of the chub, though it only lists Fyne Aire's dissertation, which we'd be mad to recommend, and *The Masters on the Chub,* sadly still unpublished, as is the voluminous correspondence between Mr. Craig Woods and this writer on this fascinating subject, which correspondence will eventually be donated to The Museum of American Chubbing, whose headquarters are on the gentle banks of the Catatonic River, one of the finest—if most neglected—chub rivers in America and surely worth a book of its own, especially if it's short.

THE LYONS ROACH

From the time I was a teenager, "Tap's Tips" has been one of my favorite columns. For H. G. Tapply is surely one of those rare human beings who can describe how to do a thing so you can really do it. Practical, sensible, and eminently clear, he yet has a voice of his own: he contributes to our store of usable knowledge and improves our fishing. He proves, month after month, that the "nuts and bolts" of fishing technology need never be mud—even if it takes a mixed metaphor to say so.

I had hoped, many years ago, to write a column called "Nick's Tricks." I wanted this more than I ever wanted to be an expert. I had a sincere desire, you see, to *help* people, not merely dazzle them.

But none of my tricks worked. Still, I had friends. So I asked for help. Good old Sparse said he had once tried to perfect a zipper for waders, so you could pee with your boots on. An eminently sane idea. But they leaked. He told me, too, how he had once often dropped his pipe into rivers but had invented a little string thingamajig that kept his pipe hung safely around his neck. Now when it dropped out of his mouth at the sight of a huge fish rising, it only plopped hot ashes into his waders.

My friend Clyde suggested helium-filled flyline, which floated in the air a few feet above the water and thus eliminated drag while dropping the fly (but not the leader) to the surface. Ingenious, I thought. But when I tried it out, an ash from my cigar touched the line and, *poof!* I watched helplessly as the largest trout I've ever seen rose to the free-floating fly and vanished forever while (and I've always wanted to say this) my reel smoked.

Barring a ready supply of tricks, I thought I might someday get my name on a new fly. Quietly, without fanfare, I perfected the Lyons Leafroller. This fly has two virtues: it catches fish and it can be tied by everyone, even cretins like me with three thumbs, two baseball fingers, and a pinky that stands at attention when the temperature drops below eighty degrees. Here's the recipe:

Lyons Leafroller

HEAD, BODY, TAIL: One inch of chartreuse polypropylene
THREAD: Chartreuse

What you do is this. First, rip off a one-inch slab of char-treuse poly (longer or shorter depending upon the size leaf rollers that drop in your area). Lay this directly along the top of the shank so that both ends hang loosely beyond the eye and curve of the hook. Then strap the thing to the hook somehow—

a couple of run-of-the-mill knots or a good wad of chewing gum will do the trick nicely.

It's a lethal fly, pliant in the water, when the leafrollers are dropping.

Unfortunately, they stopped dropping in my region four or five years ago, and although I gave several tying demonstrations, no one took much interest. No one seemed to care.

After that I lapsed into a fallow period, which often precedes the most creative days in my life. It lasted five years, four months, two days. It lasted until Vin Ringrose started to describe the pancora crab to me one day and the size trout it produced. I had seen photographs of such fish in Joe Brooks's *Trout Fishing:* ten-pounders only three or four years old.

Here at last was an enterprise worthy of my greatest efforts. I decided to start an importing firm with a Mr. Edward G. Zern called Pancoras Unlimited. We would stock a hundred American rivers, from coast to coast, with these fat crustaceans. We would increase the average size of American trout from six inches to sixteen pounds. All this would be our service to the trout-fishing fraternity. Our cut could come from sales of the Swank Panc, a new fly I was perfecting and would have in mass production by the time fly fishermen across the country realized that Trikes were out and Pancs in.

Mr. Zern and I had incorporated as PU, Inc., and were preparing to travel to Chile to snatch some seed pancoras, when the U.S. Department of Agriculture got wind of the deal and threatened to leak it out that we used worms if we did not cease and desist—so we did.

Meanwhile, Mr. Zern copped out and began fishing in exotic watering holes around the world, abandoning stateside waters to me. Fame, that whore, had so far eluded me, but it would no more. I said my mantras and went into a trance for thirteen days. On the last day, the miracle occurred. I was perched on the kitchen floor muttering when a huge, juicy roach came out from under the refrigerator, nosed around near the stove, and then climbed up my waders (in which I always meditate), and slipped into my hand.

It was a thick and juicy roach, its hard brown back glistening brightly, its body packed with leftover protein. The cities across

America were full of them. They could not be destroyed. Four appearances by the exterminator had not eliminated them from my kitchen. "Feisty little buggers," he told me. They thrived on garbage; they'd probably love pollution. The mayflies were vanishing; the caddis would probably be next. So I would promote the roach.

My mind was clear and cold now. There was an unlimited supply of these creatures in places where they were not wanted; and there was an unlimited need. They would make excellent trout food—crammed with protein and vegetable matter. *Blatta orientalis*. Or maybe *Blatta orientalis lyons*, since I was about to raise them from ignominy to glory. And there was a moral issue. The cities had been squandering river water for the last hundred years: didn't they *owe* something in return?

I took four of the pretty little things upstate one weekend and dropped them into the riffle above Slate Rock Pool. They floated beautifully, which confirmed my hope that I could create a dry Lyons Roach for dry states. And no sooner had they floated out of the riffle and into the pool then a stupendous brown trout boiled under one, took it, then came up again, smacking his lips for more.

Incredible. My fortune was assured. Did they have a Nobel Prize for this sort of thing?

I decided to proceed with caution. I wrote to fisheries management people and chambers of commerce across the country:

> *Dear Sirs:*
> *I am able to supply an unlimited number of roaches to you for use as trout food. A few, stocked near blue-ribbon trout streams, will revolutionize your fishery. May I have your opinion?*

"You should be locked up," one biologist wrote back.

"We run a clean town," said one little chamber of commerce in the Midwest. "No roaches."

I could not believe it. I had not one taker.

Worse, my letters caused alarm. Antiroach leagues sprang up across the country. Several nationally televised debates discussed whether the roach was sufficiently aesthetic—and unanimously said "No!" My college, which had been trying to sack me ever since I was caught teaching a class how to avoid drag instead of *The Importance of Being Earnest,* brought me up for charges under paragraph XXIV of the Higher Education Code, "Conduct Unbecoming." An organization called Love Your Roaches surfaced and called me a barbarian. And then Mr. Donald Zahner ended it. He threatened to reveal that I don't really live in New York City but on the Middle Fork in Idaho, and am a notorious live-sculpin fisherman, a ghost-catcher of lunkers for desk-bound honchos.

So there is no Lyons Roach today. I'd have told the tragic story sooner except that some rat, ordered to keep me mum, put Krazy Glue in my Chapstick.

THE LYONS
SUPER-FLEX LEADER

I made the long detour every afternoon because of the snakes. There was a certain convocation of them sunning on the mounds of rocks near the river, and I climbed high above their territory to avoid them. They are mysterious fellows to me. I'd like them if I could, but I can't. They turn my backbone to mush.

The detour left me breathless but was worth the trek. For every afternoon about four o'clock, three in a row, I'd been treated to an astonishing sight: when the sun slanted from the west, you could see, below the short, shallow run, where the riffle flattened and the water deepened and grew dark, the pockmarks of a dozen good fish feeding, just at or perhaps just below the surface. And if you bent your head sideways, you could see, beneath the sun's glare on the water, that a few of the largest fish even moved into the thin broken water, where they seemed on the prowl, with their tails and dorsals extending above the surface.

Though there were some tiny flies in the air—a few blond caddis, a couple of different midget mayflies mostly—I raised not a fish during this spree to my dry flies, which was all one used on this water, on three successive afternoons of fishing.

Was it the particular glare of the sun at this time of day?

Were the fish taking nymphs swept down from the pool above?

Was I using the right pattern and did it cant on the water properly?

Was my leader too large—a 5X, which was the lightest I thought would hold such huge fish, and which did not trouble the same trout in the mornings, before the sun crested the hill and fell on this run? A fish or two turned toward my flies but none came to tea. And I'd taken four fine fish from this run during mornings of fine dry-fly fishing when a #16 Sulphur was on.

On the last afternoon, though, I felt incredibly smug because, in desperation, after years of intense experimentation, the difficulty of this pool had prompted me to a last massive effort to perfect my newest and most original innovation: the Lyons Super-Flex Leader. What it is, is this: two lengths of Tibetan braided leader, dyed with goat's urine, the uppermost exactly 39½ inches long, the lower 33¼ inches, with exactly 6.37 inches of rubber band inserted between them. I had tried 103 different rubber bands until I found one of precisely the right texture and dimensions (which I will reveal when my patent is approved, for a price), and finally found the perfect way to marry braid and rubber: with a Triple Overhand, Double-Loop, Over-and-Under Smitz Knot, which I created for the job.

The function of the Lyons Super-Flex Leader, as any idiot would know, is to serve as a shock absorber at the two most vulnerable moments: when a fish takes and when it makes a sudden move. I had tried rods with wet-noodle action to solve this problem but had finally determined that the rod should be stiffer, the leader noodlier —and stretchier. Now I could use 7X tippets with absolute confidence. I could fish #22 dry flies delicately. Twenty-two-inch browns would be cream puffs, if I ever found them. The Lyons Roach had failed to make me famous and rich, but this leader would change my life. I'd patent the idea. I'd get myself sent to Yugoslavia to test it. Millions of fly fishermen would pay me a royalty on each LSFL sold. I'd get on cable TV. I'd have a video made of myself.

The final stages of the Lyons Super-Flex Leader had taken me half the night to perfect. Determination of the exact length of leader, development of the Triple Overhand, Double-Loop, Over-and-Under Smitz Knot itself (a knot that takes only slightly less than three times the time needed to tie a Bimini Twist) were historical moments. I had knelt on the living room floor late into the night, using the tip section of my fly rod, trying to get the thing to turn over just right. By three-thirty A.M. it did—but I was too exhausted to make more than the one prototype.

So, armed with this, I'd made the long detour, and on my first cast with a #22 Cream Caddis at the end of a 7X tippet, the leader turned over gorgeously, I had a good rise, I struck, and I came up blank.

The lighter leader had worked brilliantly—but I'd missed the fish. Strange. I cast back into the pod of tails and dorsals and in seconds had another good rise, struck, and again came up blank. The Lyons Super-Flex Leader was too flexible to set the hook: that had to be the problem. The rubber band ought to be an inch shorter. Well, streamside is no place to tie flies or Triple Overhand, Double-Loop, Over-and-Under Smitz Knots, so I'd have to improvise: strike harder.

Again I cast up into the run, watched the little golden dot alight and float a foot or two, then it too disappeared. I made a short, hard strike, again came up with a loose line, roll-cast the line out in a rushed, frustrated movement, could not see the fly, jerked it back hard, to bring the line off the water for another cast, and felt a sharp tug.

All fly fishermen feel a special satisfaction when they solve a difficult logistical equation on a river. Selecting the proper fly pattern and design, overcoming a stiff upstream wind, beating the drag built into twisted currents, solving a problem of approach, brings a flush of pride—and the proof is always in the catching. A slight, smug, self-satisfied smile comes to one's lips. Anything— even losing weight—is possible.

I smiled a slight, smug, self-satisfied smile. I had tried to solve this problem for three days. I might have solved it by swimming a Zonker through the pool, but that would have been like lowering the net in tennis. I'd stayed with the dry fly and my gargantuan powers of deduction had led me to the solution: the leader. I felt damned proud.

And it was a big fish, too—perhaps one of the alligators the river was known for.

Only it acted a bit oddly.

It did not go out in a heavy rush of power; it did not sulk; it did not come crashing out in a leap of exaltation and bravado. It sort of zigzagged.

This, I soon learned, was because it was not a trout.

Thirty yards out, right at the surface, I saw the writhing form of a snake, close to a thirty-incher, SSSSS-ing its way toward the opposite bank. The little golden speck that was the #22 Cream Caddis was attached to its middle, as if the fly had been dragged, quite wet, and foul-hooked the reptile.

I exerted as much pressure on it as I dared, and I am happy to report that the Lyons Super-Flex Leader worked beautifully: try as it might (and I might) the snake could not break the 7X tippet. I had created a brilliant innovation.

The constant pressure of the line and rod and the Lyons Super-Flex Leader drew the snake closer and closer. But now what to do? I was in the Rockies and I had no idea whether the snake was poisonous or not, and even if not, the closer it got the more I felt "zero at the bone." Not only could I hold an especially large catch, I now realized, but I could not uncatch it.

Closer and closer I played the snake. I gave it hard, short tugs, to bust the tippet, but the tippet would not break. I pointed the rod tip at the wretched thing and jerked, but the snake only turned and came toward me, so I promptly stopped jerking. Out it zigged and in I zagged it. Soon the twelve-foot 2 1/2-inch leader was to the tip of my rod and the snake much too close for comfort. I was sorely tempted to cut the leader where it joined the line but I didn't want to ruin my only LSFL, the prototype, and the only leader of any kind I had with me.

In desperation, I hoisted the reptile—wriggling and twisting —at rod's length and began a certain swinging, swaying motion that I thought might break it off at the tippet, launching it into space; but the 7X tippet held, and the snake kept dancing at the end of the yo-yo-like contraption, swinging closer to me on each backswing after each time I swung it out. I was furious at myself for being such a genius.

In the end, I swung it high and far, so the snake slapped down close to my feet, wriggled onto my hippers, made me dance a little jig until I stepped back into some sagebrush, and fell to a sitting position; when I saw the snake wriggle up my leg, I levitated, and booted the leader harshly. Even then it did not break. But the braided butt must have rubbed against the rocks, for suddenly, as I tugged and high-stepped, it burst, and I kicked the snake into the water and galloped downstream, making a terrible commotion.

I'm still trying to construct another leader to the precise measurements I recorded that historic night, and I have high hopes for my invention. I still think I'm a genius and I still think the Lyons Super-Flex Leader will make me rich and famous—though I don't think I'll ever to able to recommend it for the fine art of wet-snake fishing.

DISCRETE PLEASURES

SUSPENDED TIME

February and March are not cruel months for fly fishermen. Though the season is not yet open in most places, there are all manner of detailed, textured chores to be done—from tying new leaders and a few more of that new parachute Sulphur you saw, to replacing a tip-top and changing a flyline and rearranging your twenty-three boxes of flies, to oiling a reel. And in the back of your brain all the while—prompted, perhaps, by forsythia buds, then blooms—there are the first faint songs of spring.

One such hint of spring is a call, soon after the year turns, from Len Wright, who says, "Seventy-nine days." So locked in the cold numbness of winter am I that for a moment I'm puzzled. Is he speaking about some talk I've promised to give, a business date, or the tax deadline? No, it's fly fishing again—asleep for a while but now rising like a vapor in my brain, for the days until it can be practiced in my part of the world are numbered now.

Len is safe. He's going south, for bonefish, next week. Another friend is headed for New Zealand, for the first time, and I ask him to promise he'll give me a full report; still another flies to Argentina in ten days. Not for me; not yet and again not this year; but someday, perhaps.

I begin to think back to the past season, one too spare for much dreaming, though it will have to do—and pick over the few memories with nicest care. There was a sharply cold day in late April when I stood on a sandbar with Len and Bill Kelly, hoping for some fish to move; they didn't, and all I can remember is the cold, and hour after hour of casting a large streamer, and the two small fish Bill got and Len's small brookie, and the trouble, too difficult to describe, I had trying to raise my waders up over a paunch that had mushroomed.

I also remember a day when a friend and I scoured the Cats-kills, trying one favorite hole of mine and then another, trying to find some kind of action with which to start the new year. At the first we saw exactly seven flies and no fish rising, and we could pound up nothing in three hours of hard fishing. At the second I found some Hendrickson spinners in the air about four P.M. and put my friend—whom I wanted to take a few fish—on a lovely run downstream of where I wanted to fish. It was good to see the deliberate tipping up of the fish taking spinners, and I dropped to a 6X leader, put on a sparsely hackled hackle-wing spinner, and nailed the first four fish I cast to. They were the first fish of the season I'd seen rising, the first I'd caught; and this was a spot I knew well. The fish were all better than a foot long; one was fifteen inches. It was all very satisfying.

Downstream, my friend did not seem to be having much suc-cess, which felt worse for me because the guy a hundred yards below him had a bent rod every time I looked. Worrying about my friend, I cast poorly and only raised one more fish—which was properly humbling after the four in a row; then, about five-fifteen P.M., I saw my friend's rod arc and his stance shift and a good fish come straight up and fall back, and then jump twice as it took line, a marlin in miniature, going away. A few minutes later I watched the man's arm go up, the rod bend fully, the net dip down from his left hand, and the fish come up out of the water, wrig-gling in the meshes.

There is time to read a few more books before the new season starts, and I do—hoping some of it will make sense, rub off, make me a bit more skillful. Perhaps. There's always that chance. Any-way, the best of them have rivers running through them.

There is time to go to one of the new fishing expositions that have proliferated these past years, and to wander past booth after booth of irresistible goodies. I feel like a kid in a crowded candy shop and want to touch and taste everything. Especially in March. Especially when there is row upon row of new rods to flex, new flies to study, feathers from the East and outfitters from the West, old books to thumb through, and—in the midst of the great throng of brothers of the angle, many of whom aren't any kin to me at all—more of the pulse and more of the song that is growing inside.

There is a hunger for the thing itself, the fly fishing itself, as winter wanes, a desire to be closer to the rivers and lakes and their denizens, even through books and magazines, certainly through memories, even through crowded expositions. For too long, to paraphrase S. J. Perelman, I have been "two with nature."

In February and March, suspended, seeking to find ways to join up with fly fishing again, I strike up old correspondences, for I am a compulsive letter writer when the fever is upon me, and they too speak of the year past, or the year before that, or of some book or of some new leader formula that "will change my life," or how the West Branch wintered, or of planned trips or faint hopes or great expectations for the new season. And the letters, too, one to the other, ripple with the pulse of enthusiasm and dream and waiting.

The fly-fishing clubs have their Annual Days and Annual Dinners in this suspended time. They know what we need and when we need it. I go to one sponsored by The Theodore Gordon Flyfishers, and it is always a joy to see friends I haven't seen in months, listen to panel discussions and talks, see slide shows about exotic or esoteric matters, talk Fly Fishing Talk again, watch the tiers at their cunning craft, buy this or that, which I really don't need, collect travel brochures on which to fashion dreams of what might or even will be, perhaps even cast a line on the grass—still spotted with snow—near the gray parking lot, the tug of the line and play of the rhythm like an old remembered pleasure come back.

It is not a cruel time but a suspended time—a time between the solid cold of winter and the warmth and energy of a new season; now it is a time that holds a bit of both. It is a time, too, of melt—a time of bloated rivers and of dreams cut loose and race-horsing downstream. It is a time less of doing than of thinking about doing, a time not of "is" but of "was" and "perhaps" and "will be."

"Only eight days," Len Wright, aka "The Clock," tells me.

It is a time cut from the textured life of the thing itself, with the past year now fully gone and the new year still absolutely crammed with possibility, and I, anxious to meet it, wait, and then wait a few more days, another week—the season open but the flies not yet here—breathless, suspended.

NO-NAME BROOKS

Beaverkill, Battenkill, Willowemoc; Madison, Yellowstone, Big Hole, Snake; Deschutes, Feather, American—oh, and the Letort, the Brodheads, the Ausable, the Brule, and a hundred others. Magical names. Names peopled with layers of texture, story, history, legend—names associated in the minds of fly fishermen with particular men and fly patterns, with specific hatches like the Hendrickson, Michigan "caddis," "salmon fly," *Caenis*, even riffle beetle larvae. They are names to which we make pilgrimages, rivers some men hold sacred. Often too many men hold them sacred at the same time.

But there are other trout waters, found East and West, down into North Carolina and certainly in Maine. These are the little unnamed brooks that rise from springs or ponds hidden far into the pockets of wilderness farthest from civilization. These are the bright creeks that flow clear and cold, dropping, always dropping in little waterfalls, white rushes, or slow, inevitable, downward glides, into larger streams, then into the major rivers—and also into my heart.

I know one in Montana, one in Massachusetts, several in New York State, a few in Colorado, another in Maine. Some of them have local names like Otter Run or Devil's Creek, but I rarely learn them. Usually I supply my own, for most often they appear as no more than the thinnest meandering line on maps, winding back from the larger rivers like the veins of a leaf to places that are pure source. I have followed several of them this far, to the wild place, the still and steady fountainhead of what is wild, the emblem of something pure coming fresh into the world every moment. "We need the tonic of wildness," says Thoreau, "to wade sometimes in marshes where the bittern and the meadow-hen lurk, and hear the booming of the snipe; to smell the whispering sedge where only some wilder and more solitary fowl builds her nest, and the mink crawls with its belly close to the ground." Such places are necessary. They are rarely found on "name" rivers. The isolated creek is their source.

I do not hear the names of these creeks in my ears. They collect no stories but those I have lived with them—and sometimes a few I have heard from other initiates. They are not magical words but textured pictures in my brain. They are private places, so quiet that their presence is often unknown even to those who live closest to them.

Bill Humphrey lived near one—a diminutive limestoner—for five years before he realized it held trout. He got the news from a friend, who one evening, astonished, had seen a local fish-hawk coming out of the dusk with two gigantic trout. I have fished the river and taken only one small trout, but Bill, who fishes it regularly now, has had some surprising evenings there. It is an intimate, genial piece of water, which demands stealth and deft, short casts. You walk through farm fields, under barbed-wire fences. You talk with a good friend, watch the water, and never see another fisherman. Sometimes the water is merely a quick, short, shallow run, but now and then it opens into a pool with a hidden hole the size of a house for a bottom, or it cuts deeply under a bank. There are trout here, you know it—but you must be there at the right time, with the proper fly. For want of a better name—and I can think of none better—we call it Bill's Brook, and if it still withholds its charms a bit too often, we still have it to ourselves, and we still dream of finding two more leviathans, the size of your arm, in one of its deep holes. There is no rush; they will be there.

I was visiting some friends in Massachusetts several years ago, and knowing my passion, they suggested I slip away from the crowd at the house for a few hours and try the brook that runs through their property. "One old fellow catches some trout in it regularly," my host said, though, looking at the little creek, I had my doubts. It may have had a name but I have forgotten it.

I walked downstream a mile, fitted my smallest bamboo fly rod with a #4 line, a light leader, and a #18 Hair-Wing Royal Coachman. By this time I could see that it was a spritely little creek, like the Fox in Upper Michigan, the prototype for Hemingway's "Big Two-Hearted River," but small, much smaller. The greenish water flowed over white-gray sand, turned in broad bends every fifty yards or so, swept under upturned roots, under willow branches, around a fallen log. There were little pockets, eddies, and holds everywhere—but no fish working or in sight against the light bottom. I worked my way slowly upstream, making short flicks of casts, happy to be off by myself and in the water. I vanished into the tangles and deadfalls, into the steady low sounds of the river. That I caught nothing in two swift hours of fishing troubled me not at all. I could not have spent an afternoon with better company than this brook.

I was approaching my friend's house, and about ready to quit, when a voice behind me said: "Won't get 'em that way, mister." I turned, nodded, and without further invitation he continued, and I knew at once that he must be the "old fellow" who caught trout regularly here. "Only way to catch 'em on flies in this crick is to use a small black nimp, like so. There's a couple big 'uns in there, though, and that's what I'm after with these minnies. Too easy with flies, specially that black nimp. Catch yourself a mess of good 'uns if you'll just turn around quiet and fish on back down the way you come, with a black nimp, like so."

It was worth a try. The man seemed privy to the inner conscience of the brook, a man not to be ignored. Anyway, I was in no hurry; small rivers purge my soul of fret and hurry.

But while I dug out my book of nymphs, I saw my adviser climb into the pool above me and plunk in one of his baits. Had he snookered me out of his hole?

In an hour, fishing slowly downstream with a weighted #18 nymph, fishing it into the runs, into the crevices and eddies, I took seven lovely brookies.

•   •   •

Little brooks hold such charm and surprise. Though many do not seem to have defined hatches, there may be a local pattern or two that imitate what the fish feed on regularly. Such creeks welcome experimentation.

I prefer the dry fly on such creeks. I like to wade wet, with only my sneakers, and feel the cold current against my legs. Fishing upstream, I disturb the fish ahead of me far less, and I am constantly moving into untouched water, closer and closer to the source. Often the water grows smaller, and the trees and shrubs along its banks wilder, more heavily overgrown. I once followed a little Colorado creek, above Steamboat Springs, for several miles —higher and higher, through tangles of berry bushes, thistle, above a series of waterfalls, past the last remnants of a road. I slipped to the side of the stream every time I could see a pool large enough to bear the cast; I fished below every waterfall. And the tiny brookies I found were the brightest I have ever seen—with dark mottled backs, almost pitch, and red and orange spots worthy of Van Gogh's brightest palette.

I have found some startling fish in such creeks: seventeen- or eighteen-inch trout that turn suddenly for your fly with a drama —in such a tiny world—that shocks. Didn't I catch my first trout in such an unnamed Catskill creek—though by foul means? And I have found a leisurely pace, on such a stream in Montana, that was pure pleasure after the intensity of fishing several *name* rivers for a week. Far back on one of them, where a fallen spruce lay parallel to the surface of a small pool, I had to spend a half-hour working my way into position to cast for a small rainbow rising just to the far side. I finally chose a #20 Blue Spinner on a 6X tippet and had to cast sidearm, into a pocket three feet wide, under the tree. That I did so, and caught the fish in such tight quarters, was a trophy for the memory.

There are practical reasons for fishing such small creeks, too. In the early season, when major rivers often bear the greatest pressure—and may even be unfishable because of heavy snow runoff—these tiny feeders may be rich lodes. Sometimes you'll find big river fish, which have escaped the turbulent flow; sometimes you'll find fly-fishing water when the main river will bear only rougher trade; almost always you'll find a touch of that wildness you thought was lost, nearer than you imagined.

No-name rivers. Bill's Brook; that Colorado creek; a place I once called Green Trout Brook—and a dozen others. These are private places, rarely stocked, rarely fished—places with the tonic of wildness, places that freshen my jaded eye with wonder.

SPOTS

I had driven up the far side of the Madison in the early evening and parked off the road facing the river. It was mid-August and I knew the caddis hatch wouldn't start for another hour; so I got out my gear, laid it all on the hood of the car, rearranged my flies, and fussed with my leaders. I'd fished a heavy nymph on a 1X tippet that morning, and I wanted to tie on two new segments to bring it down to 4X.

The sun was at the crest of the hills—bright red and so bright on the water that I could not look at it without squinting. I'd had half a dozen or more glorious evenings at this spot. A few tan caddis would come off about a quarter to eight, I'd see a spurt or two out in the river, and fifteen minutes later the fish would work themselves into the riffle at the bend and there'd be a bacchanalian. My son Paul got an athletic eighteen-inch rainbow at that corner; I'd taken perhaps thirty fish from the riffle and eddy over the years, all at dusk, during a caddis hatch.

It was the kind of spit of land that works its way like acid into the metal of your brain. It becomes starkly vivid and it becomes yours. The heavy rush of the Madison pressed against an island thirty yards upstream, a channel came in on the near side, then everything swept past some brush at the bend and formed the sweetest little riffle, eddy, and pool you could imagine, with a flat section twenty feet wide between it and the shore. I dreamed of the spot, as I've dreamed of a dozen others. I felt quite sure I owned it.

There was a pool on the East Branch of the Croton, which I fished constantly in my teens, before I fished with flies. Mort and I were there every Opening Day without fail, sometimes with my friends Bernie and Don. There were yellow-bellied holdover browns in the eddy behind the fallen willow, and we caught more than our share of them, April after April, and we talked of the Big Bend for thirty years after we stopped fishing it, for it was *our* pool.

Someone called it a "money pool" and we used the phrase for all the others we found: one on the Schoharie, another on the Esopus, even a corner of Long Island Sound that seemed paved with fluke.

They are remarkable places, sometimes. Some happy concatenation of elements conspires to give the fish security and a steady flow of food. Unlike the American dieter, the trout is not especially interested in using more energy than he takes in. In fact he won't do it. So he lolls around these backwaters and eddies, what Al Troth calls "the supermarkets of rivers," and mooches a free lunch whenever he can. Now and then on a seven-mile float trip you'll see a dozen or so such pools and perhaps wade several of them during the day. Some, as you float, you get one shot at: one cast that must be true and properly slack, so you get that one long free drift, during which time, as you lean into the line, attach yourself to it, hold your breath, fix your eye on that tan dot of an Elk Hair Caddis, your heart is liable to levitate through your skull.

I found such a money pool on the Delaware and must have fished it twenty times, only three of which I hit it right: for a pool is not always generous but only at its pleasure. This was a Hendrickson pool and a March Brown pool and a late-evening-in-June stone-fly pool, and once, in September, I saw an alligator of a trout come up out of its depths to munch on a fat chub I'd just chucked back. At other times it might have been, for all the fish one saw, a cesspool.

I found another on the Little Snake in Colorado, one on the Battenkill, another on a little unnamed spring creek in Montana. If, deep down, you thought like a trout, or at least like a fisher after trout, you knew these spots held good and many fish. They usually provided too much protection for them ever to be fished out, and most were only generous at specific times. A thousand fishermen could try them at noon or midafternoon on the wrong day and they'd go home skunked.

My pool on the wrong side of the Madison was such a pool. I'd seen a dozen truly skillful fly fishermen try it on August afternoons and swear it was barren. But I knew otherwise. With a quiet, almost smug confidence, I knew the fish would come—so I was in no hurry. I tied on my 2X leader segment, then brought it down to 4X, then fussed through my fly box for just the right #16 Elk Hair Caddis. Then I put my waders on slowly, laced my boots without my usual frantic rush, checked my vest for extra leader material, flies, forceps, and dark glasses, locked the car, made sure I had my keys, made doubly sure I had everything I needed, satisfied myself that I did, checked again, and walked the twenty paces to the river.

A slight mist rose from the water. A couple of bats darted through the gray sky, just below the rim of the hills. Except for the steady rush of the water, there were no sounds.

The spot was exactly as I remembered it and the caddis had just started. No hurry. There were a few rises in the long flat section downstream, but I'd wait until something happened in the money pocket. In a few moments it did. I saw a spurt of water, then saw a dorsal tip up out of the slate surface, then two or three dorsals. What an evening I'd have!

I pulled some line off the reel, false cast once or twice, and dropped the fly on the inside rim of the run. I'd pick these fish off one at a time—six or seven of them: it was going to be a perfectly splendid evening.

The first fish came to the first cast and was about fourteen inches—a handsome rainbow in excellent condition. I slipped him back, cast again, and saw that the fly sank. So I poked around for my spray, remembered that I'd left it in my duffle. Since I'd known I was going to fish nymphs in the morning, I'd decided I had plenty of time to fetch it from the car and thus avoid worrying about air-drying the fly after it got darker, when I wouldn't be able to tell if it was floating or not. The car was close; it would take only a few moments.

The spray can was where I'd left it in the duffle and I found it quickly, paused to douse the fly at once, and then turned back to the river.

Two guys stood in my spot.

Where had they been—in the bushes? Upstream?

One was at the tail of the pool, the other where I'd stood. Had they watched me catch the fish? Had they waited for me to leave? Had they honestly thought I was leaving for the day?

Should I tell them whose spot it was, anyway? *Was* it my spot?
Had they been waiting all afternoon to fish it? Would they get out
if I asked them politely, explained? Did I have the right to ask
them? Was it worth a fight? Could I fish elsewhere? Was it *their*
pool? Should I at least make some nasty cracks? Should I muscle
in on them—there might be room for a third? Did I have the *right*
to get back in?

Surely they'd seen me; surely I'd taken *their* spot and they'd
been waiting for me to leave: they knew it too well. Whose spot
was it, anyway?

Ah, dear. Too many heavy questions for a humid mid-August
evening. The spell was broken. I cursed quietly. My nerves were
shot. Possession was enough of the law to make it their pool, at
least for the evening.

I watched them take several good fish as I took down my
gear, got into the car, and drove slowly down the dirt road to the
bridge. From the other side, after dark, I stopped for a moment on
the highway. I could see their silhouettes crowded against the
corner, near the bushes. They were fishing intently now, having
the time of their lives, and had probably taken ten fish apiece,
and I couldn't help hoping—against all my gentle urgings, all my
fraternal feelings for my fellow fly-fishers—that at least one of
them would fall in, break his rod, or get bitten on the ear by a bat.

BRIDGES

When I was young and could play basketball seven or eight
hours in the hot and heavy city sun, I never fished where the cars
parked. Pounded to death, wormed and spin-fished into oblivion
—that's what I thought of such places. And the outdoor magazines supported such an obvious theory: take the road less traveled
by, they advised; fish the untrammeled pools and riffles. They said
it so often I began to wonder if near hadn't become far—for certainly far was often too famous.

But it made the best of sense then and for many years; and I
took some exceptional fish in private places. I loved to explore far

back, away from the bridges, away from the telltale beaten-down grass, off into the dark of the forest, in stark rock canyons, beyond the tangled undergrowth. By my time, none of the pools I found were truly virgin; but most were not fished frequently and many not yet that season. I often found big fish in such places, like the three-pound brown in a foam-flecked pool that took me an hour to reach; and I often found those exquisite little native brookies —black and mottled, with spots as bright as wild raspberries.

Sometimes, though, the best fish were not necessarily far from the road but only took more cunning to reach. My friend Les showed me how holding pockets of no more than a half-dozen feet across could be virtually inaccessible if fished from the usual, the easy, access point. Braided currents, which produced drag; undercut banks, which could be reached but not effectively from the obvious side of the river; eddies behind rocks and fallen trees— these might be within sight of a thousand fishermen who *thought* they could fish them, though only one in that number had the imagination to make the difficult wade to the other side—from where—and only from where—the water could be fished fruitfully.

We fished one of the most accessible spots on the Gallatin one day—with a parking area large enough to be a used-car lot. Everyone and his grandmother must have passed that gorgeous pool, stopped, made thirty or forty casts, caught nothing, and moved on—convinced, perhaps, that it was *too* pretty and obviously pounded to death. But Les urged me into a position three-quarters across the stream—which took ten minutes to negotiate—and from there I could cast directly upstream along the opposite, highly visible bank. You wouldn't believe the number of fish we caught.

Yes, we used a finer leader tippet than most people would have chanced for such broken water, and he produced a killing fly pattern; but I've fished that same pool ten times, with the same fly and leader but from the common side, and caught nothing. It was our position that was decisive.

It's axiomatic that there's a whole lot more water in a pool, and many more places of security for a trout, than most of us imagine when we look merely at the surface. "Far" can be quite close—but just as difficult to reach as trekking a couple of miles back into the hills. And I'm beginning to think that the far which is close is more challenging.

Sandy Bing likes swamps. He likes the impossible cast into the tiny pocket amid the complex of weed and tangled brush and branches. Twenty fly fishermen might have paused at the spot, gauged their skill against the problems of the cast, contemplated the lost fly, the wasted time, the tinge of frustration, the tying on of a new fly, and said, "No thank you. Not today." I've seen Sandy take huge wild fish from such lairs; since he uses only one or two fly patterns, it's surely the place and the presentation that make the difference.

Bridges are usually the nearest access we have as we pursue our fate along rivers. We pause at them, take our first view of water for the day at them, launch our boats near them, but too frequently pass them up. I used to love bridges—covered bridges, painted barn red; small old bridges with clanky wooden boards; concrete and trellis and steel bridges. I caught scores of trout near and under them in my early teens—when I had less mobility and knew there had always been a hatchery truck there a week before. There was a dark, deep quality to the water: shaded from the sun, fetchingly shadowed, deeper for the pilings and eddies, slower, troutier.

Then for many years I ignored them. They were too obvious, too handy.

Last summer my friend Justin met me in West Yellowstone and wanted to fish the Madison for the first time. It can be a humbling river, even when you know it well, and impossible when you don't. We met at seven, on a dark drizzly evening, and scooted down to the Raynolds Pass Bridge. We had our rods but no waders, and we didn't intend to fish; it was too late and the storm clouds were too heavy, but from the vantage of the bridge I could show him what I'd learned about fishing the edges of the Madison current, the pockets—how to avoid the heavy flow with the dry fly and turn what can look like a massive, unvaried rush of tumbling into more manageable, readable, smaller strands.

The rain was pelting when we reached the bridge. Though we had no rain gear, we hunched over and ran to the southeast corner, looking upstream. I was all teacher. Note, I said, how just fifteen feet above the bridge a riffle pinches between two rocks and forms a little glide-pool. The fish will be just *there*, where the broken water grows a trifle flatter. Of course there was nothing in *this* pool—it was right near the bridge; I just wanted to show him the principle. You shouldn't fish right near the bridges, I counseled, and he nodded.

And then there was a little spurt of water just below us.

"Did you see that?" I said.

He hadn't.

No matter. The fish rose again, this time rolling, probably for a caddis, so I could see—and *feel*—its size. A good fish. Justin saw it this time. Bred for fly fishing on eastern fish, he hadn't seen many like it and became excited. Me, too.

Then the water was silent for five minutes and we got to thinking it was a freak until, in the midst of the raindrops, we both saw the big fish come up two, three, four times in a flurry of feeding.

"That fish can be caught," I said.

"Do you think so? Do you really think so?"

"Absolutely. It can be caught. It's going steadily—"

"The rain, too."

"—and I really don't think we should pass it up. We shouldn't pass up that fish. It can be caught. Justin, that fish can definitely be caught."

The rain had already drenched us to the skin and we were cold, but we didn't hesitate to trot back to the car, grab our rods, and rush back and then down the embankment.

The fish not only refused my #14 Elk Hair Caddis but went down and wouldn't come even for the few naturals that now fluttered near the surface. Well, that was that. We'd missed it. But the rain stopped for a half-hour and we fiddled around above and below the bridge, from the shore. Then the rain started again, heavier than before, we came back to our first spot, I managed to tie on a #16 Elk Hair in the near dark, and a fish promptly took it.

I told Justin to try but he insisted they were my fish; I'd spotted them: I'd made the brilliant discovery that a smaller fly was needed. It's nice to have generous friends.

In the next twenty minutes before impossible dark, I raised four fish in that little look, the largest well over two pounds, and in my excitement, lost every last one of them. Justin went back twice that week and caught five big browns and rainbows from that corner. He was sold on bridges.

Me, too.

BIG RIVER, LITTLE RIVER

It has been said that the river makes the man—that it molds his style and character as surely as it wears its will into the earth and rock through which it flows. The limestone and chalkstream build slow stealth, cunning, minute care. Broken water builds quick reflexes, a restless ever-moving eye. Burly water draws forth a love of force, rough challenge, raw adventure.

I am probably not many men but simply not man enough to master any one type of river. Or I'm pathologically restless. I don't know. But my pulse quickens as surely to the heavy rush of the lower Madison as it does to the delicate flat glides of a carrier on the Kennet. Do not ask me to choose. Push me off in a MacKenzie River boat a bit above Varney Bridge and I am at once intensely alive. The guide rows out into the center current and then a bit further toward the far bank, and my liver flutters. My gear, in order since daybreak two days earlier, goes insanely haywire from my nerves. The lines from both rods jam and tangle. The fly has slipped from its keeper and is in an argument with one of the leaders. I nearly tip the boat.

Then all is clear.

A few false casts and the orange Elk Hair Caddis—the size of a cherry tomato—sets down two feet from the rock shore sliding swiftly upstream.

"Closer," the guide says.

"I know."

And the next is closer, barely half a foot from the bank, and it miraculously floats—high and bright, an orange spot on the slate and riffled water to which my eye is glued—ten feet, then twenty, then a few more, and then it drags. Quickly I cast again. We are passing so much good water. The eddy behind that boulder is there then gone. I miss the undercut bank off to the left. Shall I fish above or below the fallen tree? Can we go back? Can we stop? It's happening too quickly. And the water ahead—a full day of it—is also full of promise.

Amid the bubbles and the floating bits of debris and the foam, my eye fixes on the bright orange spot again, and this time it doesn't float four feet before that slanting form, its spots huge and its mouth stretched open, leans up into the fly and my arm jerks upward and I feel its heavy force against the current.

It's a day with fifty such moments, each a little different, and I can't get enough of them. Late in the afternoon, not because I'm bored and want something exotic but because it's the right way to fish in that water, I slap fat black Girdle Bugs into eddies and undercut banks and still more browns bust up madly after them.

Do not tell me this is "the jockstrap school of fly fishing" or merely an idle game for tourists. It's fly fishing. And it's as exciting as any brand of the thing I know.

But is it more satisfying than an afternoon on the Kennet?

Neil Patterson and I have left the others at the hut and wandered up along one of the carriers that flow out of and then eventually back into the main river. It is a small piece of water, a miniature canal let to go wild, with rubble bottom and water only faintly amber. Across the carrier and thirty feet upstream, there is a little irregularity: an end branch or two of a fallen willow just out into the flow and there is a little eddy upstream, then a short break where the water quickens to scurry around the impediment and make up for lost time. Directly downstream there is a tiny backwater. The minute target is no more than three feet in any direction. And target it is: a good brown is alternately rising in the eddy and then the same fish seems to be falling downstream and taking flies gingerly in the quickened break and even to the head of the backwater.

"Is it one fish?" I ask.

Neil insists it is.

He says, too, that the trout can only be caught if the fly is cast—with a slightly left-hand hook—behind the willow branch.

But not too far behind. Then it will catch in the branches.

All is immediately clear to me: I cannot possibly catch this fish.

"But of course it can be caught," says Neil.

"Not by me."

"Try it."

But I insist it's his fish. He saw it first and he's earned—by virtue of being *able* to take it—the right to try for it. Anyway, I've taken three fish that day and am satisfied, and I insist—quite truthfully—that I enjoy seeing a tough fish caught by a truly skill-ful angler quite as much as, or more than, I enjoy catching one myself. This is odd but so. So I sit myself down in the tall grasses, with a box seat for the action, to enjoy myself.

Neil goes down on one knee and inches his way up a little closer, his wild red hair barely a foot above the grasses and his shaggy wool sweater—into which he hooks all his flies—half-hidden. Then the rod comes up straight and the fly loops back near me and goes forward, and falls like down in the breaks. Too short. But the water bulges a foot above it and the trout comes downstream in a rush and my heart takes a crazy flutter and the fish swirls and misses.

"Gone," I say.

"That fish can be caught," says Neil.

"He's spooked. You won't take him for three weeks."

But Neil waits ten minutes, then casts again, a little up-stream, perfect. Not a nudge. He casts ten more times, then changes his fly, then changes it again to a cockamamie hairy thing he tied up that morning, then changes it still another time five casts later.

"That fish can be caught," he says.

I lean back in the grass, look out at the Berkshire fields that Constable might have painted, dream about Montana and the fat Kennet brown I caught that morning, and now and then look upstream at Neil. He hasn't budged from that spot. I'd have got cramps; I'd be stuck there for life.

An hour later I see the fly land for the tenth time—impossi-bly—where it should, stall in the eddy a half-second, begin to move, and vanish in an explosive bulge. The brown is a bit more than three pounds and I am limp.

• • •

Big rivers, little rivers. Each has its own delights. In the end, I guess the river doesn't quite make the man but the man seeks out the river to draw forth something in him. "Every object rightly seen," says Emerson, "unlocks a quality of the soul." And since most of us live lives that are a bit too drab for the best inside us, and go to rivers to unlock much that lies dormant most of the year inside us, we like a variety of waters. We say we like the "experience" of a particular river. We like the sweeping bends of the Delaware, the stillness of a Pennsylvania limestone, the exquisite challenge of the Battenkill, and the generosity of the Yellowstone in the Park when every last cutthroat is on a caddis binge; we like a pert mountain brook and a raging western river; we like rivers we've fished a hundred times and those we've fished only in dreams.

Lately, I've been dreaming of the Deschutes and the Rogue, and of a little creek in the east Catskills that drops through a clove for five or six miles. I've dreamed of fishing that creek for more than forty years, since I was a kid and every summer drove up the road that skirts the clove to my grandfather's hotel. I've dreamed of wearing sneakers, taking a single Sucrets tin of little Hair-Wing Royal Coachmen, and a sandwich, and fishing that little creek right up the mountain, to the falls and above. Who knows what qualities such a trip might unlock?

"Will you fish it with me next summer?" I ask my friend Emile. "All of it—from the valley to its source?"

"I know that creek," he says. "The bed, from Haines Falls down, is nearly all slate. I doubt if you'll find a fish."

"None?"

"Maybe a few little brookies that got washed in from the feeders."

"I've always wanted to fish that creek," I say quietly. "Does it make any difference . . . that there are no fish?"

"Well, yes, old fellow, I suppose it does," says Emile. "But let's fish it anyway."

POCKET WATER

Art Flick always liked the pocket water best. Quick, hearty, vigorous in his movements, he hopped onto the rocks, found firm footing where he could, his eyes always searching little runs and glides and eddies behind and between the boulders. Something in him responded to the quick movement of the water. Several times he told me he was bored by the slow water that I was growing to love. Fixed in a likely spot, but never for long—for he was a restless, busy fisherman—Art always cast rapidly, his fly dancing up into the runs and riffles, riding so high I could frequently see it from a high bank above the water. Usually he used his beloved Gray Fox Variant. He almost always took fish. I saw him take six from some pocket water on the Battenkill, at midday, in June, when no one takes fish. And he certainly always had fun.

Pocket water has it special delights. It is not "exact imitation" fishing and much of it is coarse and close, not fine and far off. You are looking for likely water mostly, seeking a place a trout would seek, where it can get food and safety. You are watching a vibrantly alive surface, braided with twisting currents and swirls and bubbles and eddies. You are looking for a patch of water a couple of feet around, and you have to make quick decisions to get your fly above it, so the fly will float into the pocket. You move quickly because you probably need only put a fly across a pocket a half-dozen times to know if a fish will take it. Floats are brief, strikes quick.

Most times you fish the water, not the rise. But I have seen great pocket water come alive when a good hatch is on, usually one of the larger flies. I've caught a Green Drake hatch on two very different rivers, both with great pocket water and brisk riffles. I'd see a spurt rise, then another, then fish to those spots and almost invariably raise a fish. When fish in such water are on the feed, they can be gluttons.

I like pocket water best when the water has dropped and

there are true pockets behind exposed boulders. Looking upstream, there may be a dozen or more spots in any lateral section
of stream, several of which can be reached from where I stand.
The casts are short and abrupt mostly; your eye is constantly darting from one pocket to another, and when the cast is made, trying
to pick up and follow the quickly tumbling flies from among the
thousands of sparkling bubbles. I like to wade wet, with a good
pair of felt-bottomed sneakers, and feel the rush of water around
my legs. I like to travel light and use only a Hair-Wing Coachman
and a Gray Fox Variant, or perhaps a grasshopper, if they're on.

Much of the Neversink River in the Gorge is pocket water,
and the few times I've fished it have been a delight. In some
stretches there are thirty pockets to pick in that many yards of
water; in another, the river pinches and runs hard up against a
shale wall with a crown of rhododendron, and the pocket is forty-
five feet across and deep. The water is pale green and clear, and
when the water is not too roiled on the surface, you can see the
lunge of the fish fractions of a second before the strike.

I like a section of the Willowemoc that's like that, too—one
exposed rock after another in a three-hundred-yard stretch, and
when there are grasshoppers in the field and I'm fishing a Jay-
Dave's Hopper, well-greased and riding high, every pocket seems
to have its resident (and greedy) trout.

The Esopus has great pocket water, and for some reason the
Hair-Wing Coachman is especially effective there. Preston Jennings fished the pattern a lot and told Arnold Gingrich about it.
Arnold figured the fly imitated something; I'm dubious—but it
sure takes a lot of fish, and my old eyes can see it as it bounds
downstream above me.

I've had some wonderful days on the Esopus in recent years,
thanks in good part to the untiring efforts of Ed Ostapczuk to save
it. I have never known a man to work harder for a river—or earn
better and more convincing results. I used to avoid the Esopus—
dreading its discolored water and crowds. But whenever I'm
nearby now, I try it: it's a great pleasure in the late summer to
work upstream with a Hair-Wing Coachman, flicking it into every
run and behind every rock, watching the spurt rise of the wild
rainbows or the more deliberate take of the increasing number of
nice browns.

Of them all—the rivers with lots of pocket water—I think I like the Gallatin best, up in its narrower regions, especially when the grasshoppers are on. This is leisurely fishing, wandering up the meandering, fecund river, fishing its bends and riffles, looking for feeding lanes along the far shore and eddies behind the rocks and deadfalls. The fish do not run especially large—up to fourteen or fifteen inches, honest count, with an outsized rainbow tossed in now and then—but they are bright, wild, eager fish, and an afternoon of watching them charge up for a high-floating hopper can be a tonic for a weary soul.

Fly fishing can get pretty fussy, even arty sometimes. I happen to be mad for such difficult spring-creek fishing lately, where the precise cant and silhouette of a specific *Baetis* imitation may be critical, where I have a chance to catch a truly gigantic brown that I've stalked for an hour, on a 6X tippet and a #18 or smaller fly. In such fishing you really must fish fine and far off, and your casting had better deliver the fly as lightly as thistle, or you're out of the game. You really must offer your quarry a fairly close approximation of what it's taking for tea, or it won't be the slightest interested. You must think about your position and the trout's and the float of the fly and the particular brand of Pale Morning Dun you are offering at four P.M., and whether the fish can see you from its position, and whether you can cheat and use a size larger tippet, which will surely hold it, if you've been skillful enough to bring it up, which you probably haven't. It's careful fishing, slow fishing.

It's an addiction that truly hungers when most it satisfies.

Pocket-water fishing is different.

It's more rest than challenge; it's simpler, more elemental; it's a happy couple of hours. You cast in under the rhododendrons, in the shadows of that far pocket. A plump March Brown comes down and is taken, the flash of the fish slightly to the right. You mark the spot, cast quickly sidearm, the fly moves briskly and you must adjust the line for drag, or potential drag, and then there's a little curl of water, a rise with a sound, a *thwunk,* and the heavy turn of a good fish.

It all happens very fast.

The cast, the roll of the fly on the rippled felt of the river, the pressure of that live thing on the other end, abruptly, as it turns against the current: it's a terrific way to fish—and a great antidote, when the lovely pastime of fly fishing threatens to degenerate into an art form.

DUSK

Sometime after the first full heat of summer falls, fishing shifts to the extremities of the day. Dawn and dusk are when the river is most alive, and there are times when a pool, even in the dead of summer, hosts a bacchanalia.

I used to fish the morning hours most frequently at this time of the season. I'd start while it was still dark and fish on into the first bright hours of midmorning. Often I'd fish a large nymph or streamer downstream in the chill of dawn, with the features of trees, hills, and farmhouses slowly emerging through the early-morning mists. There were big fish to be caught at such a time. I remember a huge brown slowly turning for a streamer as it raised up high in the currents below me on a Westchester County stream. The fish was twice, three times the size of any fish I'd taken from that river and much larger than any I'd ever seen taken from an eastern river. More fish and much bigger fish were on the prowl at that early hour, and often it was like fishing a different stream.

In July, with barely any light in the sky, I used to fish the broken water of the Esopus, with stone-fly nymphs, for that fly hatches in abundance on that river, but always at night. The specific fly is the *Perla capitata*, perhaps half the size of the giant salmonfly out West, and using a smaller version of Charlie Brooks's stone, tied in the round, and Charlie's deep-nymphing technique, I often took three or four good rainbows.

But lately I've been drawn to the other end of the day. Perhaps it's the pleasure of being cooled and refreshed after a long, hot day of summer. Perhaps it's because the dry fly, at least for me, is so much more effective at that time—and the fly I always prefer to use. Or it may be that I'm growing shy of those early-morning jaunts and simply like that extra hour or two of sleep. But perhaps it's that something in the dusk stirs or touches something in me at this moment in my fishing life. Fishing can be like that: a matching of your rhythm to the rhythm of the kind of fishing you do. There are times when nothing but a raw float trip down a heavy Montana river will suit my needs, or fussing around with some terribly shy trout in a crystalline spring creek, or fishing a mountain feeder or a defined hatch on classic old Catskill water that I've gotten to know well. There are rhythms to a fly fisherman's year, to his life, to a day; there are rhythms to a cast, a drag-free float, and each section of each discrete river a fly fisherman ever fishes. Fly fishing thrums with harmonies.

Lately I have been powerfully attracted to the rhythms of dusk fishing. The sun begins to slant farther from the stream. Distances blur. A certain chill enters the air. Shadow and substance commingle. And sometimes, when you catch the river just right, a river that was a dead board all day is pocked crazy with a dozen rising fish.

I caught such moments twice on British chalkstreams. Both days had been long and lazy, with few fish visible and none "on the fin." With the local prescription of not casting other than to a visible or rising fish, my right arm had practically gone numb from disuse. Then the sun dropped below the Berkshire hills, that day on the Kennet, and suddenly the river was lit with a haunting gray light. I stood at the tail of a long deep run and in succession saw one, then two, then six or seven fish start to feed, their circles suddenly spreading out from the slate surface. I chose the nearest fish and it came at once to the little brown sedge. Then I took another, then a third. The river was hushed and there was no wind. The fish that had been so shy all day—a shyness that was more than what is called being selective; they were nearly dead—were now cream puffs. The same thing happened on the Test, after a terribly humbling day, when a Rusty Spinner fall made me think it was a different river—almost an overcrowded ghetto.

Such success is enough in itself to recommend dusk fishing. There are times of the year, times on a particular river, when the fish are simply most active—or *only* active—at dusk. Spinner falls, a hatch of big cream *Potamanthus*, half a dozen late-summer caddis-fly hatches—often the only decent fishing of the day is when these evening hatches are on.

But there is something else: big fish.

Often they lose all caution when the sun is off the water, especially on western waters, where they feed less at night.

I'd gone with Don Kast, Les Ackerman, and a batch of guys to a private run on the Gallatin a couple of years ago, and we were all stretched out in various spots, fishing to a patch of water in which literally dozens of fish were working. There was no need to move; you worked your way into the place you wanted to be, and you could fish without moving a foot for an hour and not exhaust fish to cast to. I was with Don on a long flat glide, using a #18 red-bodied spinner, and he was catching a slew of fish while I watched and fumbled a bit and finally got the hang of the currents. We didn't get out of the water until after nine, and by then I'd had my fill of good fishing. We'd gotten no truly large fish, but it had been a perfectly splendid evening or so and a few rainbows went up to fifteen or sixteen inches.

When we got back to the car, one fellow was missing—and when he came up he was cursing like mad: he'd been fishing a huge sculpin imitation on a 1X leader, saturating it with fly dope and floating it into the heart of the heaviest current. Something had come up, taken the fly in a heavy swirl, turned a couple of times in the current, and then stormed downstream like a runaway train, breaking the line. The guy was in shock. He'd never hooked a fish that large.

"Serves you right, fishing for muskrats," said Les.

"Bring some cable next time," said Don.

I always think of such big fish when I fish at dusk: fish as big as a dog, coming out of black depths, to nab your largest fly. But it is the quality of the fishing that intrigues me most: the rapt, magical quality of that last hour or so before dark. The river seems more alive, the sense of time is suspended yet hurtling toward some peak moment. No matter that it now takes me six or seven tries, the fly held up to the vanishing light, my eyes squinting, to thread a hook; no matter that I can often only watch the general vicinity in which I've cast and cannot see the fly on the water. It's growing darker, second by second, the fish are working and may at any moment stop, and I fall into a hypnotic, even mystical state, astounded by remarkable happenings. On the East Branch of the Delaware one night, I suddenly looked up at the sky and saw a gigantic swarm of stone flies, more than I'd ever seen in the East. The sky was thick with them and the birds were dipping and darting, and then I bent my head and looked at the surface of the water: everywhere in the riffles you could see the tooled turn of rainbows, porpoising, not leaping but turning in arcs, everywhere, wherever I looked, like martens or minks or something truly wild, come out only at a witching hour, and I simply stood and watched them, for twenty minutes, one with the mists, narcotic of riffles.

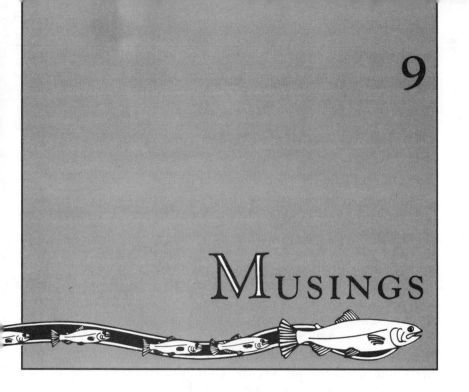

9

MUSINGS

THE SNOBBISH
FLY FISHERMAN

To most other fishermen—those who use bait or lures or cheese or corn—the fly fisher is a snob; to fly-fishers who also spin or plug cast or fish with bait, the person who only fly fishes is a snob; and to some fly-fishers who fish all kinds of flies, the dry-fly purist is a snob. But there are snobs and there are snobs. And a true snob is a snob is a snob.

Fly fishermen often use delicate equipment; they can discuss fly patterns and leader tapers ad infinitum; the peculiar flanged tail of someone's Hendrickson spinner is critical; they study entomology and brood about the morphology of rivers. Fly fishermen probably read more, and with a more discerning eye. They must be aestheticians as well as hunters. The fly-fisher's sport demands more of him—and he knows this. He is generally less interested in how many fish he catches than in how they were caught. Because of all this, the philistine's cry of "Snob!" may well be met with more than a trifling sense of superiority.

A snob thinks he is better than his neighbors. He may think himself "better" by virtue of his wealth or intelligence or schooling or friends or breeding, or because he carries a fly rod instead of a minnow bucket. Sometimes he *is* wiser, and wisdom is a value I prize highly, and I willingly want to learn from him; but most wise men I have met are too wise to be snobs. There's *no* value in outright snobbery. The snob looks down from an exalted height— either in utter seriousness or, hopefully, with merely a touch of whimsy and playfulness: frankly, it's fun to be a bit snobby now and then.

But within the broad ranks of fly-fishers, there are levels within levels of its own brand of internecine snobbery, some of it no fun at all. Howard T. Walden, that gentle man, says in *Upstream and Down*, "I know of no sport so ridden with taboos, so gangrenous with snobbery, so reeking with cant, as trout fishing." And yet all of that book and all of *Big Stony* chronicle the ways of fly-fishers that are deeper, broader, wiser. I have seen and heard the taboos, the cant, the snobbery, and also the vanity, the peacocking, the breast-beating, the *mucho macho* act, and it always seems so silly. Some fly-fishers abhor those who fish in lakes, or with wet flies or streamers, or with dropper flies or in salt water. One titan of the dry fly sincerely confessed to me: "There are those of us who still take it very much to heart that George LaBranche ended his days a *bone-fisherman*."

Alas.

Yet why "Alas"? Has not this gentleman every right to fashion his own demanding ethic of what the fly-fisher should be? Of course he does. For himself. I may think, with Walden, that it smacks of "the faint reek of decadence," I may see a certain crankiness in a particular purist's position, but I admire demanding men who raise the net a bit in the tennis game, shorten the endlines. It's their right and it's their challenge to play by the most demanding rules. But I, who am cut of rougher timber, like more space around me when I play: a court that allows me to use more of my resources. There are other honest delights in the broad world of fly fishing. G.E.M. Skues heralds one of them in a lovely little lyric that includes this stanza:

Let the Purist rejoice in the fly that he dries,
And look down on my practice with hauteur,
  But for me the surprise
  Of the flash of the rise,
The rosy-brown wink under water.

And I rather prefer not to be thought a cretin because my fly sinks. We each fish for our own discrete purposes, out of our own sense of the pursuit.

Yeats says, "Arrogance and hatred are the wares/Peddled in the thoroughfares," and I would rather see them peddled there myself, rather than along the rivers I love and even in certain "exclusive" clubs that carry snobbery to its inevitable and logical end: bigotry.

But Yeats goes on in that poem, to ask: "How but in custom and in ceremony/Are beauty and innocence born?"

Custom and ceremony—the very bulwarks, sometimes, of snobbery—are also, often, the most joyous aspects of fly fishing. Whether it is the local, personal ceremony of an Opening Day brunch or the celebration of a three-hundred-year-old tradition, we often cherish most deeply such repeated forms in our fly-fishing life. And conversely, what icons would that happy iconoclast Len Wright shatter if there were none? Part of the pleasure in all of Wright's books comes from the very fact that there is some custom and ceremony in fly fishing to be broken. Custom and ceremony do not make the snob, nor even *bad* breeding, but arrogance and hatred do.

Yet the dry-fly fisherman who, from that exalted height, looks down with serious contempt upon the nympher is quite different from the fly-fisher who finds the latest Hawg-Bass Ho-Down a bit barbaric. Fishing by the clock, for pound and number, against other superstars of the Hawg-Bass circuit is, on any just scale of values, a desecration of the sport. Fishing is not a competitive sport, at least not as I undersand it, nor are its rewards so easily tangible. The very existence of tournaments encourages this mentality.

Fishing with a wet fly or nymph, fishing in lakes or in salt water, may not be someone's cup of tea, but they don't rank *lower* by any values I can find. Fishing the dry fly happens to be vastly more pleasure for me than fishing wet flies, but someone else's wet-fly fishing troubles me not a whit—nor, necessarily, do I feel *bound* to fish the dry fly, contaminated if I do not. (If someone hauls out limits of fish or fishes across my line or steps in ahead of me in a pool or shouts, I'm peeved: but all that falls into the category of toilet training and I would scarcely call myself snobbish for resenting someone's excremental mischief in my neighborhood.)

It is surely one of the great delights of fly fishing to see a trout rise to your fly, but sometimes only sinking flies will move the bigger fish, or even reach them, or even reach *any* fish. There are times when *any* fly will fail to reach any fish—and at such times one is faced with the further choice of using bait or lures or dynamite, about which we winking snobs do not speak here. Imitating the natural insect upon which trout are feeding brings me much more satisfaction than merely luring them to an attractor pattern, because you have had to live so much more deeply in the trout's domain, solve the riddle of its feeding. But I also enjoy popping a little bug with rubber legs away from a rocky shoreline for smallmouths or quick-stripping a Marabou Muddler on a Montana float trip. I like strawberries and roast beef and escargots and sour pickles and a couple of dozen other dishes, too.

I would argue long for the increased pleasure one would find in fly fishing, or in certain types of fly fishing—the increased challenge, the greater tug on one's resources—but I would scarcely dream of telling my neighbor to eat worms before he used a *sinking* fly or fished for *bonefish*. And though fly-only stretches have distinct management potential, I am reluctant to tell the thoughtful spin fisherman to keep his distance; I would rather *persuade* him to try the fly.

I like to fish upstream with a floating line, but I would resent being told, say by the British, that this was the only "fair" or "honorable" way to pursue trout. Why should it be? Yet I do not resent restricting myself to one fly, without a dropper, or stubbornly insisting to myself that I catch a particular trout, on a particular stretch of water, on a dry rather than a wet fly. Extra flies are clumsy—they're liable, even in my hands, to catch two trout, and they often tangle.

I doubt if fly-fishers, who are mavericks and should remain so, will ever accept a single code of ethics legislated by a Central Committee of High Priests. Nor should they. If we really fished with a fly because we thought it made us holier, we ought to have taken up fasting, self-flagellation unto sainthood.

We fly fish—at least I do—not because it makes us "higher types," members of an occult snobbish clique, but because it is more fun that way, more demanding. Like Yeats, fly-fishers are fascinated by what is difficult. We throw fish back—at least I do—not in some elitist illusion, but because they may then grow to a worthy size. Fun, challenge, commitment to preserving our quarry and its habitat should be the foundation of any fly-fishing code. Which need never make us snobs.

THE INTENSE
FLY FISHERMAN

There was a time, some years ago, when I could fish with terrifying intensity. Give me a western lake and even the slenderest odds of hooking a ten-pound rainbow on a fly, and mules could not pull me from the water. From dark icy mornings until long after the sun bled beneath the sagebrush hills, I'd cast until my arm was numb and sun had baked the ridges of my right forefinger, wrist, and thumb a brilliant, blotched red.

I did this not once but dozens of times. I did it East and West, in Iceland and on British chalkstreams.

Sometimes I caught fish, sometimes I didn't. If I got some, I wanted more. If I got none, I had to hook a first before I left the water. If I got small fish, I wanted alligators. If I got a big one, one beyond my hugest hopes, I thought there might be another, even huger, down there. I lived merrily, mindlessly, uncomfortably on the fringe where fishing bleeds away into madness.

Such intensity led to fierce family fights and, much worse, I thought, botched fishing. The rush of blood heavy in my head, I raged around the waters, an indifferent caster, a diffident loner. I knew little about bugs and could not be bothered to learn. At its worst, I lost my love of new and remembered waters, my wonder at the quick dart of a trout for a fly, the fun of good fellowship and a common language. Only the intensity—dumb and manic— mattered. It positively wore me out.

I had forgotten why I came to rivers in the first place. I had forgotten the meaning of the Duke's gentle words, from *As You Like It:*

> And this our life, exempt from public haunt,
> Finds tongues in trees, books in the running brooks,
> Sermons in stones, and good in everything.

There was, for a time, only the hot pursuit. But then, for whatever reasons, I swung to a far more leisurely frame of mind. I found I could stand passively behind a friend and chuckle as *his* fires raged out of control. Once, on a lazy little British chalkstream filled with wild browns anywhere from fingerlings to five-pounders, I spotted a fish rising just downstream of a river point topped with overhanging grasses. As the current zipped around the bend, swirled back behind the point, it brought a conveyor belt of easy food to the safe fish, which was dimpling steadily. Fingerling or five-pounder? I could not tell, though the protected lair suggested a smart, large fish.

Maples and willow on my side of the river made casts to that far bank quite impossible; there was enough current in the center to assure drag; and a cast above the point, from below, could only bring the fly whisking down past the trout's cafeteria. The rules of the river prohibited downstream fishing and that wouldn't have worked, anyway.

The one clear way to manage the classic little problem was to wade across the deep center current and cast to the fish from directly downstream. On a western river, with chest waders, I'd have done it even in my most leisurely, laid-back frame of mind. But I wore hip boots, practically the best suit of clothes I owned, and the only suit with me, and I'd caught a few fish already. So I sat down on a rock with my back against a maple and was content to watch.

After a few moments, my host came around the bend. He is a great enthusiast for fly fishing, a builder of business empires, a man not ever to retreat from a challenge.

"There's one, near the point," he whispered loudly. "Oh, he's a good one. Oh, he's a very *verrrrry* good trout."

"I've been watching him," I said.

"Well have a go at him, Nick. Have a go at him. That's a *verrrrry* good trout."

"Not for me," I said. "Not today. He's all yours."

So my host got in and I leaned back against the tree to watch. He cast beautifully—a long line, hooking off to the right. But try as he might, he missed the corner by a foot, dropped his fly above and watched it sweep away from the eddy, picked up drag, got his fly caught in the willows behind him, came finally within inches of the eddy, and then stepped back and shook his head. The fish would not budge from that spot, not an inch. And my host *had* to catch it.

Sooner or later, I knew, probably sooner, he had to wade across the river in his hip boots. I felt quite smugly sure of this point.

He inched out toward the current and watched the water line rise on his boots. He cast again. Short. The angle was all wrong. He could not resist it, I thought. He *had* to have that fish. He was gut-hooked by that trout and could not possibly resist going after it.

And he couldn't.

A few minutes later the poor builder of business empires was sloshing helplessly across the river, soaking his Harris tweed jacket far above the pockets. And then, just as he got to the far side and prepared to cast backhanded up toward the fish, the trout stopped feeding for the day.

I was merciless toward him, for I had been there myself, many times: I had fished late into the night when my marriage hung on the slenderest of threads; I had waded into a pool in a jacket and leather shoes; I had walked through muck as treacherous as quicksand and waded on nights so dark an owl would have gotten lost.

But I was sad and envious, too. In my new contemplative

height had I lost some of that marvelous passion that is also part of the sport? Of course I had. Fly fishing was never a purely contemplative recration. There are times when, if you don't commit your full soul, if you don't put your blood into the pursuit, you might as well be playing a quiet game of cribbage before the fire. Isn't one of the prime reasons we venture out to *use* that intensity coiled within us?

Still, I was talking to Charlie Brooks about fish passion once and we agreed that certain symptoms of it could be lethal. I mentioned the guys on the Great Lakes who had died of salmon mania when wild weather came and they would not leave the water. He told me about a guy who'd arranged to float the Madison during the salmonfly hatch. Ten minutes after the boat pushed off, the sport saw stone flies everywhere, and fish taking them. His casting grew wild, and with some help from a Montana gust of wind, he managed the unique distinction of being probably the only man to hook himself with a Sofa Pillow through the bottom lip and up into the flesh of the upper lip. Pinning his mouth shut. The guide wisely saw at once that this was a bad scene and announced that he was heading for shore and would hustle the guy to a hospital.

There was a loud, determined noise from the sport. The guide thought he must be in great pain and rowed harder toward the shore. There was a louder, raucous, this time intelligible: "*Nooooooo!*" The man adamantly refused to leave the river; he *had* to finish the float.

"That's a real fisherman!" a friend said quietly, nodding approval, when I retold the story.

A *real* fisherman?

After eight hours on the water, the man had caught a dozen good trout but his face was distended beyond recognition, infected, and he was in a state of acute shock. The guide rushed him to Bozeman and doctors were barely able to save his life.

What intensity!

What lunacy.

TWO BY TWO

I once knew a young woman from Texas who had left her husband and two children and lit out for a life of her own. Her family thought she'd gone bananas; friends loathed her for her irresponsibility, or lack of heart or independence—whichever you choose to call it. But she told me that when the menfolk went coon hunting she had to sit and sleep in the back of the pickup truck, on and under burlap bags, half the night, with the hounds. This could not have been much fun. On a recent trip to the Rockies I heard of three passionate fly fishermen whose wives had bolted. It sounded like an epidemic.

But on the same trip I saw—or mostly, heard—something of a very different order. I had walked a couple of miles down the Henrys Fork, to escape the mob, and had had a pleasant August evening of fussing over some very fussy rainbows. I'd caught five or six fish, none too large, and had lost one that made me shake, and I was tramping back through the high grasses along the near bank to meet some friends at the parking lot near Last Chance. Looking upstream, I could see no other fishermen to the first sweeping bend. But as I came around the turn, I heard several animated voices and walked closer to hear what they were saying. The two figures, out some twenty yards, the only people I could see on the wide expanse of dark water, were both young women, perhaps nineteen or twenty from their voices. One was hunched over in the classic "changing the fly" pose; the other was casting. The caster was using that high-arm downstream cast, with the defined stop-line gesture, that is so familiar—and potent—on the Henrys Fork and upper Yellowstone. She was managing the maneuver expertly.

One of them, it must have been the caster, said: "There's another. They're not on the dun. I had a couple of bumps but that was it. They'll take an olive floating nymph. Use a number twenty. Hurry up. There are dozens of fish working now."

"You sure it's the nymph?"

"Definitely the nymph. Right in the film."

I watched their silhouettes for four or five minutes, listened to their animated talk, and almost rigged up again when both rods arced and I heard them both laughing. Forty minutes later, after I'd changed out of my waders, put away my gear slowly, and compared notes with my friends, the young women had still not come back. Their car and mine were the only ones left. For a moment I worried about them. Then, thinking of their enthusiasm and obvious skill, I knew they were quite all right and happy as larks, and praised the brave new world that had such creatures in it.

Of course there are thousands of female fly fishers these days, and more every year, who would never be asked to sleep with the hounds, who have no mind to leave their husbands, and who fish with skill, pleasure, and passion. Evie Haas and Gwen Cooper, who wrote the charming *Wade a Little Deeper, Dear,* love to fly fish and do so all over the world. Phil Wright told me that Mary Rentschler, well into her eighties, loved nothing better than to float and fish the Big Hole. Joan Stoliar, Barbara Worchester, Ann Pettine, Barbara Lewis, Jackie Mathews, and scores of others are fly fishers—there is no "man" or "woman" about it. It's not so important that Joan Wulff can outcast and outfish just about any man I know—fly fishing really shouldn't be a competitive sport, anyway—it's that she loves to fish and for every good reason enjoys being on the water. She may have decided to take up fishing and casting because otherwise—she once told me—she was fated to row her father and brother around the lake, but she does it now because she loves it. And for years she's encouraged and taught other women (and men) to fly fish, many of whom are now great enthusiasts.

There is a photograph of Theodore Gordon, otherwise virtually a hermit, with a handsome young woman in early-twentieth-century dress, and he happily reported that his best fishing chum was a girl. Mac Francis dedicates *Catskill Rivers* to his wife, Ross, *his* "best fishing chum," and having seen Ross fish several times, I know Mac isn't being overly modest when he says she's a better and more enthusiastic fly fisher than he. You see more and more couples on the water together these days and I find that a happy sign. I've seen Dwight and Leslie Lee coming off the Henrys

Fork arms around each other, and the cover of one issue of *Fisherman's Luck*, the Boise Valley Fly Fishermen's fine magazine, shows a man and woman kissing in midstream, framed by overhanging trees, her flyline trailing in the current languidly.

Two by two they came into the ark, male and female, all living creatures. Oh, brave new world, indeed!

It's all so pleasant and even romantic to contemplate—this breaking down of sad antique chauvinist values—that, closer to home, I've been tempted several times to try to convert Mari to the sport. Twice, recently, in fact, I've done an astonishing thing: bought her a Montana fishing license. Of course these times were before float trips down the Madison, and they were more precautionary than with much expectation that the licenses would be used; but I had my hopes.

She fished on neither trip.

The first time down she read James's *The Portrait of a Lady*; the second she mostly watched the gorgeous, changing scenery. I enjoyed having her near at hand and I *think* she had pleasant days, at least until the hailstorm the second trip. But I know in the deepest part of my heart that she had absolutely no desire to fish. She does other things, she tells people who ask her whether or not she fishes; she happens to do them quite well.

So I have resisted the temptation to try to interest her in it all. We can kiss elsewhere. If by some wild chance she decides to join 'em, which I doubt, I'll help. But I'd bet against it.

I have in my mind an image that tempers all the romantic feeling stirred by these pictures of women in waders. I was sitting on the bank of the Battenkill with a friend's wife, on a lovely autumn day some years ago. She had on the Authorized and Proper outfit and had carelessly laid a new Orvis bamboo rod in the high grasses; I think she had been given the rod for her birthday.

"What a perfectly splendid morning it's been," I said. "Two fish. A couple of misses. A bright September day."

She looked quickly at me, turned away, and said nothing.

"The air's been so fresh and it's lovely to be out of the city for a . . ."

"I don't think it's 'lovely' at all," she said slowly, and I saw her

reach out unconsciously and grasp the tip section of the fly rod.
She grasped it rather roughly, I thought.

I looked sharply at her. She always went fishing with Peter: I
thought she loved to fly fish. There had been times when I envied
him like mad.

"Do you think I like this?" she asked. "Do you?" And before I
could answer she went on for a full fifteen minutes about the
stupidity of it all, the discomfort, the waste of time, the interesting, worthwhile, and educational things she might have been
doing in the city on such a *lovely* weekend.

Off the wall as such a position might be, I knew this opinion
was indeed held by some sad souls; but I had never expected it of
her. I reached over quickly and removed her hand from the tip
section; she had been crunching and bending it brutally.

"You shouldn't be here, then," I said gently.

"It's *your* fault!" she said.

I flushed bright red.

"Peter keeps saying, 'You don't want to be a split family like
the Lyonses, do you? Oh, I've tried, so hard, but the truth is: I
love Peter and I absolutely loathe this silly, horrible, dull game of
his, this *fly* fishing."

There was no reason why she should pretend to love it, then,
I said. Mari and I do many things quite happily together; others
we do separately. And as an afterthought: "You'll loathe it less if
you don't feel you have to do it."

"Do you *really* think so?" she asked, and her voice was so
eager, her smile so bright, that I knew I'd carelessly spoken some
of the truest words of my life.

STILLNESS

Where I live they bludgeon you with noise. If it isn't the
grinding of subway wheels—steel against steel, raucously, doing
violence to your ears—it's the long, thin whine of the siren, the
wild beat of the hand-held radio blaring, the pounding of the
jackhammer, the doing of deals.

Nor are some nearby trout streams better. Often they are crammed with clusters of people who like to be near other people who fish. There's often much shouting. Many of the shouts are convivial but loud. Many are in Latin.

I cannot understand this any more than I can understand why people would enjoy linking the worlds of fishing and competition. I happen to be a fierce competitor and I am a fan of fiercely competitive sports, such as football and boxing; but I simply cannot get fishing and competition into my head at the same time: the one is personal, intense, essentially private—the other is a spectacle, sometimes with a cast of hundreds.

There are the big, garish bass tournaments, of course, with flotillas of ten-thousand-dollar bassboats (bedecked with gadgets, bespeckled with gold and silver spangles), rushing out at daybreak to do battle with bass—and with each other. There are hundreds of saltwater tournaments, and walleye tournaments, and lake trout derbies; somewhere in Long Island swims a bluefish with a twenty-thousand-dollar bounty on his nose; the biggest and most fluke on most party boats are still worth a couple of hundred bucks as high hook. And now there are also fly-fishing tournaments. England, long home to match-fishing for coarse fish as well as refined chalkstream fishing, has either upgraded the former or degraded the latter to include trout on a fly. After the first international tournament the winner was photographed with his slew of dead trout laid out on the grass like corpses. He'd gotten a lot of them. No doubt about that. They were big fish. He was the clear winner.

Even, somehow, had they returned all trout as they were caught, I cannot think of a game I'd like less to play: catching trout by pound and number, where I was assigned to fish for them, and when, for a prize, for honors, by the clock.

The clock is crucial. In fact, all trout fishing has been for me a disciplining of my inner clock. In my early years it ran haywire: I rushed and fidgeted and allowed everything and anyone I was with to control the tempo with which I fished. I kept saying I had gone to the rivers to be free of the city-clock and the city-noise and I often found myself controlled by them two thousand miles away. Fly fishing has been for me—along with much else—a pursuit of discipline, a pursuit of some phantom and elusive stillness, tied

somehow to a stillness in the natural world and to mastery of a
fluctuating series of skills and to development of character. It has
been connected in my imagination to a special sort of fellowship,
beside rivers and far from them, though always with fly fishing as
the hinge.

Give me one good friend, with whom I can share notes and
an ethic, from whom I can learn, whom I can watch (since we
can't watch ourselves unless our egos rise up out of our skulls and
look down as we cast, which one would believe to be the case in
some instances of elevated egos); let us talk quietly and fish a
stretch of water together or apart; let us not talk too much, and let
our words imp the happy rhythms of our fishing, slip between
times casting or watching water, noiselessly. Let me row ever so
slowly down a long stretch of shoreline in an old wooden rowboat,
with a good friend casting a fat hairbug in against the deadfalls
and lily pads, into coves of pickerelweed and to the sides of dark
stumps. I can make a morning or an evening or any stretch of
timeless time at all, doing that. That's one of the great pleasures
on the water—being with a good friend; but I can't think of much
as unpleasant as several long days I've spent with noisy fellows,
full of braggadocio, bringing competition into everything from
their brilliance with Latin terminology to endless scores with our
speckled friends—last year, two weeks earlier, that very morning
while downstream, out of sight.

I was alone with a western guide once—a noisy chap who
kept talking about noisy, incompetent eastern dudes who
thought they knew how to fish. I was incompetent all right but
I didn't claim otherwise, so he talked to me. The fellow put me
in a run to fish the dry fly upstream and then, to my astonishment, fished downstream toward me until our flies hooked. It
was a day of furious emotions and the worst possible hopes on
my part that he'd fall into a muskrat hole and break a leg.
What happened was merely that he busted his rod—a new
early-model graphite that exploded on what I thought to be an
extravagant double-haul. I practically cheered. We were miles
upriver and my emotions were not sweet as I lucked into a
half-dozen good trout on Whitlock Hoppers while the poor guy
pretended not to notice. Later he stewed; I merely gloated and

would have traded all the trout and certainly all my venom for a day on a barren eastern creek, alone.

Mostly I retreat into a thick shell I've built for myself at such times and simmer in certain memories. There is one so simple that I scarcely know why it comes to mind so often—practically nothing happened.

I was fishing some popular public water in the East, and to avoid what was becoming a crunch of a crowd, on a Sunday in mid-May, I kept walking downstream until I was well beyond the last brother of the angle, half a mile in from the road or more, and had come to a wild patch of country, protected by bramble and deadfall. I had fished the pool before and knew it was not one of the better spots on the river, with too much slate for its floor and not enough depth for fish of any size. But I saw a ten-incher rising steadily along a far bank, and then another, a bit larger, in the tail of the pool, under an arching willow.

My immediate instinct was to pick them both off quickly, first the one in the tail. They looked to be accommodating trout.

Then where would I go? It was midmorning; I was to meet my friend at one o'clock. We had rushed up from the city early, and before we'd met the crowds, I had managed to take two small fish. The day had started fast, and I had carried my city-clock in my nerves—fishing rapidly, even carelessly. Then we had seen the crowds begin to form and I had walked past three pools I'd wanted to fish, each with two or three fishermen in it, two of whom said there was plenty of room for another.

So I sat. I found a well-placed rock and sat stark still for an hour, watching the pool and the little wilderness around it. I saw some suckers grouped on the bottom, a couple of dace, an occasional caddis fly dancing on the surface. There were several orange trout lilies pushing through the green on the opposite bank. Now and again a swallow swooped down the alley of the river. A couple of Gray Foxes hatched and fluttered off; I noted that this was precisely at eleven thirty-one. A chipmunk came down to the mossy rock near the head of the pool, sniffed, flicked its head nervously, touched the water with its nose. The trout rose a dozen times and I let them rise, watching their position each time, the riseform, their resting spot high in the water; on and off, they both rose the whole time I was there. The sun angled through the trees and rose higher. I sat disembodied and watched for an hour and then another hour and then still longer.

I watched and lived in another world.

I saw no one and heard none of the cars on the highway and did not say a word.

It was beautiful.

TO KILL A RIVER

I have written several times of a certain gargantuan brown trout that rose to take a foot-long chub I'd caught and released. It was a glorious fish, perhaps eight pounds, in excellent condition, and I have dreamed many times of its sudden appearance out of the depths of that huge bend pool, its leisurely turn, the way it took the chub sideways in its mouth—its spots and hooked jaw no more than two feet from my eyes—and then retreated slowly to the bottom of the pool.

I have dreamed many times of that trout, and of the bright cold river in which it lived. Dimly, in a gray city winter, the fish would rise in my brain, flash its challenge to me, then disappear. On certain particularly grim days, "in lonely rooms"—as Wordsworth has it—"and mid the din of towns and cities," I chewed on that dream for sustenance.

Oh, I was quite aware that the fish might already have been caught. Hadn't I seen a determined crew of men with minnow buckets and stout spinning rods head off to that bend one night with flashlights, when I was putting my fly rod back into its tube? Surely there were far better fly fishermen than I who knew that hole—they might have taken the fish fairly, honorably.

It might well have migrated to another pool in late autumn or shifted with spring floods.

Or it might have died. It was clearly an old fish, the last of the old grizzlies in that particular corner of a besieged wilderness.

I knew all this. But still I dreamed. There was always a

chance. And dreams need little more than the faint hint of possibility to survive. I have lived on less.

I knew also that the trout's world might die, for I had seen many rivers killed in many of the ways man has found to kill rivers—channelization, logging, pollution, dam-building, road construction, and by fishermen themselves, through overkill. When, as a teenager up from New York City, I fished the East Branch of the Croton River in the 1940s, it contained many hold-over trout of substantial size. Within a few years after the spinning reel became popular, the river was virtually put-and-take. Along the banks of another river I fished twenty-five years ago, there are now nearly fifty tract and trailer homes; I cannot fish it anymore.

When I first went to Montana, I was astounded at the fecundity of the rivers; but I heard then that forty years earlier the fish were twice the size—and one guide *boasted* to me of having stacked trout from the Madison in wagons each fall like firewood. I saw a raft-load of fishermen come off the Madison during the salmonfly hatch with a boatnetful of huge browns and rainbows, caught when the fish were most vulnerable, on live stone flies fished from a spinning rod and a plastic bubble; they must have had seventy or eighty pounds of trout between them and were going to make another trip, illegally, for another limit. Even the West cannot bear that kind of pressure—and Bud Lilly's fine catch-and-release concept is surely as important as legislation keyed to prevent the destruction of the rivers themselves. Even if the rivers are protected from pollution and dam-building and other physical destruction, they will be of little value if they have no large wild trout in them.

What is it that we truly want? Certainly not hatchery fish, no matter how large; certainly not merely a lot of fish, if they provide no challenge. We want a touch of the wild, the chance for the unexpected, a connection to cold, bright rivers in which quick, selective trout feed our dreams.

Dreams. How many ways they can die.

"Last week," Ed Van Put wrote to me in August, "we had a fish kill on the East Branch of the Delaware below your Bend Pool. A friend picked up a beautiful wild brown of 25¼ inches, which he found dead. Perhaps he was the one that took your chub some time past?"

Perhaps.

"Anyway," Ed continued, "he was without a doubt the love-liest brown I ever saw. Unfortunately the East Branch does not now receive even those intermittent cold-water releases, and when temperatures go into the high eighties, only Mother Na-ture's hand can step in and revive that river. One of these days we will solve the injustice."

Niggled to death by lukewarm water.

What a way to go.

Not Kepone, not PCBs, not sewage, not road salts, not any-thing overtly, obviously scandalous—but negligence. For years the City of New York has had reports that a minimum conservation flow would not take one drop of water from the city's needs, but bureaucratic red tape has so far foiled the best efforts of fighters such as Dr. Bernard Cinberg, John Hoeko, Frank Mele, Art Flick, Harry Darbee, Dr. Alan Fried, and others in a fine organization called Catskill Waters.

How dreary the conservation fight must seem to so many fishermen. They have little enough time to fish, and the whole entanglement with meetings, hearings, complicated legal proceed-ings, and biological studies of rivers must seem too painful or bor-ing to claim their time. Though the numbers of those in the fight—from California to the East Coast—have grown over the past ten years, they still represent a minuscule proportion of those who fish and have a vested interest in the life of rivers. I can only think they're bored by the issue—or fail to connect it with the result: dead trout, dead rivers.

Or perhaps they hope vaguely that someone else will do the job for them.

Mele is a violinist and a writer. To the best of my knowledge he finds committee work and meetings and litigation a painful process; he'd rather fish, make music, write a novel. He'd rather be with a few close friends than a hundred men with a cause. But much of the impetus and groundwork for Catskill Waters has come from his efforts—and there are others, across the country, who (like us all) would rather fish than meet, but who have become crusaders, fighters.

Surely the fly fisherman is on the front line. That brown trout that fed my dreams is, like the canary in the mine, the first warning of danger. The nonfishing conservationist sees the physical damage to the river, the community rises up when they fear typhoid or Kepone. The fly fisherman—who not only fishes *into* the river but wades within it and must understand its biology if he is to realize its treasure—comes in every way closest to its heart and spirit. He sees first and he must act first.

The river has always been a metaphor for life. In its movement, in its varied glides, runs, and pools, in its inevitable progress toward the sea, it contains many of the secrets we seek to understand about ourselves, our purposes. Siddhartha found life and meaning in rivers. Norman Maclean, in *A River Runs Through It*, is sustained by the mystic web and spirit of rivers. Haig-Brown says: "Were it not for the strong, quick life of rivers, for their sparkle in the sunshine, for the cold grayness of them under rain and the feel of them about my legs as I set my feet hard down on rocks or sand or gravel, I should fish less often."

Without rivers, we will fish not at all.

To kill a river is to kill our sport—and our dreams.

Perhaps forever.

10

SEASON'S END

LAST DAYS
ARE FOR DREAMERS

To be perfectly safe, I saved two days with which to end the trout season: a Thursday and a Friday. I wanted to round off the year; I wanted some long hard fishing, away from the crowds, and some active trout. I wanted a tidy chord or coda to end what had been a very pleasant season—and two days, before the busy last weekend, would be private and surely safer than one.

Last days always held surprise, high drama: a day in October on the Big Hole when every trout in the river wanted my Dave's Hopper for lunch; a late afternoon on the Ten Mile when trout after trout—you would not have believed the river held so many —busted up at streamers I had chucked to them; and that cool evening on the East Branch, three casts from season's end, when an alligator of a brown, bigger than my arm, rose to take a huge chub I'd tossed back carelessly. Mysterious, wild, memorable things happened to me on the last day of a season.

Perhaps it was the onset of the cold, the start of the spawning mania, or the intensity with which I always fished at season's end. I thought of a dozen such days, filled with excitement, as I drove upstate on Thursday, watching the autumn color grow richer, denser amid the green, as I headed north, toward trout country. Gash of scarlet, yellow of beech and maple, oaks red and tawny, the sun bright and cold, and I, at middle age, still trembling, like the kid I've always been about this fishing business, full of hopes and dreams.

But the Willowemoc was pinched and shrunken, clear as water in glass; the trout were skittery phantoms, quick dark shadows, and all I caught was that image in the pond of all the colors of the mountain doubled and blurred, so there wasn't any recognizable form, only an abstract of color, a late Monet or Guston.

I was scarcely discouraged on the long trip back to the city. I still had Friday. It had been a long full year and I merely wanted to give it a coda, a tidy ending.

The Willowemoc had been too low, but the Neversink in the gorge would be perfect—a brilliant choice: when the water dropped below the tops of the boulders there would be thousands of pockets, and the cool weather of late September would have the browns fighting for our flies. I picked up my old friend Sandy in the rented four-wheel-drive and we met Justin near the Neversink at ten-thirty. I was achy and tired from the trip Thursday but no matter: I'd fished the Neversink twice this year and had grown to love the broad tumbling river, studded with boulders and long glides, tucked into the base of a deep, narrow, primitive gorge. The trout were wild browns, there were reports of four- and five-pounders in the deeper pools—and there was a wildness about the place, with its dark forests and huge stands of rhododendron and mountain laurel, which in May and June had been in luxurious bloom. The property belonged to Ben Wechsler and we were grateful for the invitation.

Our plan was to take the four-wheel-drive a couple of miles downstream, then trek downriver another mile or two and fish up. Then Justin would drive the car upstream another mile and Sandy and I would fish up the last stretch to him. I couldn't wait.

"You shouldn't drive so fast," Sandy said as I whipped up the rutted dirt road, anxious to be there, to be on the water.

"I'm crawling," I said.

"I'd hate to get high-centered," he said as I scraped over a

stone, "and have to walk back and get a tow truck. I'd hate to . . .
SLOWLY, Nick!"

A turtle could not have been going more slowly.

"Slow and steady. SLOW-LY," Sandy said.

"You really ought to be more careful, Nick," Justin said.

"I'd just like to get there," Sandy said "I've been *high-centered*
—rock, *rock*"—a deep sigh—"I've been high-centered in some
ugly places, some very ugly places, Nick."

So I crept at a ridiculous pace and we inched closer and finally got there and suited up and headed down to the river. Perfect. It was precisely the right level. It was clear but the little rain
the night before had given it a touch of color; it was low, but this
was a river that fished best in lower water. I had absolute confidence that I'd made a brilliant choice. Justin said he'd gotten six
the week before. We'd get sixty today.

The gorge was dazzling and I paused a couple of times—when
Justin erroneously thought my heavy breathing was a sure sign of
too much middle-aged paunch—to look at the fluttering birch
and beech leaves, yellow and ocher, and the umber slopes, where
tawny browns mingled with the remaining green. The bottoms of
the pools were peppered with yellow and brown leaves, and I
hardly noticed that the slight morning sun had given way to a
chill gray and a steady drizzle.

When we'd gotten downstream as far as Justin thought I could
walk, we each settled into a pool and began to cast. In a moment I
forgot the fluff of scenery, the chance of putrid weather, and concentrated on the tiny tuft of white that was a Hair-Wing Royal Coachman flicking up into the head of the pool and drifting down through
the bubbles and foam of the Neversink. There ought to have been
one there, and one there. I fished four pools hard and never saw a
rise. So I switched to a Dave's Hopper at a gorgeous bend pool, where
the white water bounced around a turn, washed in against a huge
rock wall, eddied, and then shot downstream around a boulder. The
twists of current and crosscurrent made it hard to keep the fly afloat,
but I kept flicking the grasshopper in against the rock, hoping so
large a fly would draw some alligator up from the depths of the
beautiful pool. On the tenth cast a respectable brown, about sixteen
or seventeen inches, darted up out of the opaque depths, turned,
swiped at the fly, which hesitated for a moment, sending that brisk

charge of electricity up into my hand. Pricked and gone—but I cast a dozen times anyway and then headed upstream.

The gray and drizzle had settled in for the day, and I figured it was the lousy weather system that was keeping the fish down. I waded the rocky pools with more difficulty now, tripping several times, falling flat on my face once, tossing my rod up onto the grass as my foot hit a submerged rock and I fell forward, caught myself, banged my knee, and barely kept myself from a full-fledged dousing, which, in this weather, would have been disastrous.

By the time I got to the spot where we'd left the car, I was exhausted. Sandy, my age, looked little different in shape from what he'd been thirty years ago, when we'd been in the army together; Justin, twenty years younger, was a mountain goat. I was tempted to volunteer to drive the car to the spot upstream where we'd all agreed to meet, but I had some last faint hopes that I'd raise a good one in the final stretch. Anyway, Sandy was afraid I'd high-center the car, especially without his sober counsel.

As I worked my way upstream, the weather grew more and more foul and my high hopes changed to grim determination: not to collapse before I got to the spot upstream. I cast poorly. I passed up difficult pools. I tripped and stumbled and trudged wearily upstream. And at last, beyond the final bend, I saw Justin, high on a rock, cross-legged, safe, reading. He'd caught nothing, but his happy enthusiasm was undiminished: he'd fish the river all autumn; he'd snowshoe in during January. Sandy had caught four or five, raised a few others, one of decent size. He was humming.

My score was less impressive: seven flat-out falls, a busted reel, a broken net, a bleeding wound like a stigma on my forehead smack between my eyes, a knee that felt like mush, bruised ribs, a back that ached so sharply I thought I'd be hunchbacked for life, a dribbling nose, two boxes of soaked flies, a wet sandwich, shin splints, and one small brown trout, about nine inches.

Without a word I stumbled up the hill to the car, disengaged myself from my fishing gear and from the season, and headed glumly for the highway, happy only slightly that we hadn't been high-centered.

Sandy, a tiger on the stream, began to doze; my mind grew furiously active. I dreamt of the bruised ribs and bleeding forehead that were the only coda I'd have this year. And as I race-horsed back to the city, I dreamt of a first day in April, only half a year in either direction, when dun Hendricksons popped up out of cold, slate waters and rode the currents like little sailboats into the safe harbor of my dreams.

IN A TACKLE CLOSET

The season has ended. There was not enough of it; there never is. Did I once actually write: "Fishing is nothing if not a pastime. It would be hell if I did it all the time." Now, in October, having fished too little again, still with the tug of angling in my veins, with good memories but somehow too few of them this year, with some dreams of meeting certain hatches I never met, I think I could do it every day, fish, most of the day, forever.

But this season is shot, and I am left only with those memories and speculations, some dreams that are never less than bright, and my tackle closet. It is tackle time, and I have skipped off by myself and hidden in my tackle closet, where I keep fussing around, touching, making lists, remembering.

The snake guide must be replaced on my #8 glass rod. Taking it down one afternoon at the pond, I pulled too hard, my hand slipped, and I ripped the thing off—and put the lower end of the guide an eighth of an inch into my index finger. Idiotic thing to do. The mark is still there. And also the mark, and sporadic sharp pains, on my heel, after that long day of wading with a torn sock.

I take out all the rods I used this year, about eight of them, old friends. There's the big #10 graphite I tried for the first time in the spring, on a small eastern trout pond. "Didn't know there were tarpon here," a man said, smiling, shaking his head. I had gotten the big weapon last winter and had wanted to try it out. A big, very powerful weapon. I used it with a shooting head, the first I had tried, on the pond, and I was astonished with what it could do. It heralded new worlds, a greater reach. So what if I didn't get to fish big western lakes or salt water with it this year. I had the thing now; I knew I could use it; I trusted graphite finally, years after everyone else, as always, after having seen two busted, four years ago, on mere backcasts. It was light and it was remarkably powerful. My fish dreams were expanded by its presence in my closet. Tools beg for use, and I had added a new tool this year, one that augured possibilities.

Several glass rods had served me well: well-balanced journey-men of our time, modestly priced now, durable, pleasant to fish with. Not only could I not fault them: I realize, wiping them clean of some mud, that I had used them more frequently than any other rods this year. Cleaning one of the smaller rods, I remember that the last time I had used it, I told my companion John Taintor Foote's hilarious story A Wedding Gift, in which the bridegroom sacrifices one wife for one legendary brook trout named Old Faithful. "That's nothing," said my friend, and he told me of an elderly gentleman we both knew, who, many years earlier, had taken his wife to the North Woods on their honeymoon. After they had been paddling for several hours, working hard because a three-day storm was predicted and the rains had already started, the guide called out that he had forgotten to tell them something: his shack had burned down. They'd all have to sleep in a tiny one-room cabin together.

My companion stopped.

"Is that the whole story?" I asked.

"Yep."

"Well, what happened after that?"

"Nothing happened, you dummy."

Then there are three rods, made of bamboo, and as I check windings and guides, wash cork handles lightly, look again at certain inscriptions, pen markings on them, I know that, as objects, I would never lose a speck of my affection for them. These are older than the others, two of them quite storied and priceless; touching them makes me shiver. Are they *better* tools? How would one judge "better"? More useful? More delicate? More durable? In some ways. At certain times. And they are certainly better to have *off* the stream: they cheer, thrill, delight me; the feel of them is the feel of something alive, vital, with something of the maker still in them. I worry about them, as I never worry about the others; I handle them like fine china; I remember threats to their health, the source of this nick and that scratch. I fish with them less lately but I love them as I have always loved bamboo. They are not snob-objects, not effete, not old-fashioned, not obsolete antiques. Each is the fruit of some one man's art, skill, imagination, patience, craft, and heart. Each is different. In a world where most things are the same, that alone is a lot. I admire them for themselves and for certain specific kinds of fishing they do best and I use them with a special pleasure and I want to protect them. Someday I want to make a piece of prose as useful and lovely as a fine bamboo fly rod.

There are some bad cracks in one floating flyline—happily one of my few last double-tapers; I'll cut off the bad end and see if I can make a shooting head from the rest. I want to learn a few new knots and splices this winter, and this five-year-old line will be my guinea pig. The other lines, like so much of the best modern equipment, had held up well; they need little care—only wiping down. I clip the last few inches off two, and build loops—which, stubbornly, I still prefer to nail knots: I've seen professionally tied nail knots pull out, and I find it easier to fasten a new leader to a loop.

The vest goes into the washing machine; the fifteen-year-old fish-jacket goes to the tailor, for dry cleaning and sizing—it will last another fifteen if I can hide the ragged thing from my wife. The hat, which I prefer frumpy, remains scrunched in the corner of the closet. The nets do not need repair this year. The reels get a very light oiling and then go back into their chamois bags with their spare spools. The waders were new this year, and Phil gave me a new right rubber with aluminum cleats to replace the one I left in the mud; in a month or so, some wintery evening, I'll punch holes in the sides of the rubbers so I can run a shoelace through them and secure them to my ankles.

An old flashlight gets dumped. It's four years old, corroded. A few flies go out with some frayed leaders. I ship a fly box and some flies, which are serviceable, but not for me anymore, to a young friend who will be glad to give them a new life.

And then I turn to the flies.

Boxes and boxes of them.

Home-tied and store-bought; Whitlocks and Flicks and Greens and Bedinottis; some stone flies Merrill tied for me and some striper flies Steve made in the Midwest and sent to me, which I haven't yet used; some Tapply hairbugs I had hoped to use in Maine this June (a June that vanished) or on Tap's lake; some of my good friend Thom

Green's Leeches, which British friends called hairbrushes and which dozens of stillwater trout, in the East and abroad, could not resist this year; a Woolner mosquito larva; a score of Thom's Damn Greensels; delicate midges, outlandish Sofa Pillows, sleek little nymphs, and bushy Woolly Worms. I still have more than a dozen of Del Bedin-otti's superb Hendricksons, thorax tie, which I'd got in a trade for an old Hardy Perfect reel, and a few funny Bitch Creek Specials and Girdlebugs from that Montana trip—was it really two years since I had been there?—and some of George Bodmer's Colorado Kings, which worked everywhere, and a last Boyle shrimp and two last Leiser Llamas.

I clip leader remnants from a few, fluff a few others, sort them, disengage some lamb's wool from a few barbs, put them in boxes and tuck them into their corner of the closet.

Then on the floor in a back corner of the closet, I find the little pharmaceutical box, with wire fasteners, that Flick used to send me a dozen Gray Fox Variants for Christmas last year. For all the madness the Christmas season brings to New York—with its mad crowds and madder buying sprees—I'd have it come twice as often if it came with such little boxes.

In the dark closet, in October, I finger it and put it on a shelf. Such a little box, filled with emblems of a craftsman's skill and heart, simple and elegant little delights and eminently useful in their day, made by hand at a time when most hands only turn knobs—such a little box, empty now, a bit crushed, found by chance in the dark corner of my fish-closet in October, is the first harbinger of spring.

WINTER DREAMS
WITH SPARSE

He walked into my life fifteen years ago, with his pink face and slight stoop, with his three-piece charcoal suit and quarter-inch-thick glasses, looking like an antique gnome or a tax collector. His first words to me were an angry growl. "You can't use it,"

he said. I didn't have the slightest idea who he was and told him
so. "Alfred W. Miller is who, and if you think you're going to use
my story 'Murder' in that blasted anthology of yours, you've got
another thing coming to you, buster." He liked to punctuate with
"buster."

Interspersed with those growls were long, marvelous talks,
perhaps in the great leather couch in his beloved Anglers Club
before a bright log fire, both our suits burning in a couple of places
from hot cigar or pipe ashes. One minute he'd introduce me to a
gigantic mutt named Mange, who could perform amazing feats
with food and devour the refuse of his entire ambulance detach-
ment in the mud and bivouacs of France in 1917, the next he'd be
railing against salmon fishing, because when *he* caught a fish, sir,
he wanted to know why the beggar took the fly. Sitting there,
chuckling away, in danger of being burned to a crisp, we used to
vow that someday we'd go winter camping together. He was tough
enough to have done so, well into his eighties; I was the cream
puff.

He had a thousand tales. A dozen times I heard him tell the
long, rambling, hilarious "fly in the nose" story, about a friend who
got a Fan-Wing Royal Coachman caught in the tip of his nose on a
Sunday morning in Pennsylvania, and though he always carried a
tackle box filled with a thousand gadgets, he could not find one with
which to extricate himself; the story progressed to a diner, where a
waitress was terrified by his odd nose-dress, and then to the sudden
discovery that his car was on fire; then a rattlesnake somehow
appeared mysteriously, and finally—an hour after he'd begun the
tale—his friend tumbled down a hill and knocked the senior
member of the Parkside Anglers Association nearly senseless—
twice. He had tales about Mr. Hewitt, whom he had known well and
loved and always called "Mister," and LaBranche, Roy Steenrod,
and the Brooklyn Fly Fishers; he had serious reservations about
Theodore Gordon because the man had abandoned his sick mother.
Sparse's other nickname was Deac, from Deacon, for his moral
uprightness.

He was adamant one June when I told him I had not yet been
on the water. It was a disgrace. He growled and promptly hauled
Mari and me off to the DeBruce Club on the Willowemoc. We
fished a little together—he was a deft left-handed caster—and he

showed me where LaBranche cast what he called the first dry fly on American waters. Then he said, "You've been working too hard. You need an uninterrupted couple of hours on the water to refresh yourself, bub. I'll entertain your missus." And he sat with Mari at the kitchen table in the Krum farmhouse and told her, in great detail, for four hours—the information being somewhat more than she wanted—about ballistics and maneuvers on the Mexican Border Patrol.

He was astonishingly precise about a great variety of gadgets and contraptions, some in common use, some of his own invention—like the zipper for chest waders and the attachment that kept you from dropping your pipe into the drink. No matter that the former leaked and when the pipe slipped it only dropped hot ashes down your waders.

I'd heard the "fly in the nose" story a dozen times and I was at the lunch table five years ago when Sparse began to tell it, faltered, and his great memory failed. I did not tell him to tell that story the last time I saw him, on his ninetieth birthday. Frail, shrunken, he had lost over eighty pounds. Hoagy Carmichael had rigged him a hat with a wire brace screwed into the cloth so that he could hold a pipe in place without using his hands and not incinerate himself; the old guy loved the idea of it. I wanted to hear Sparse tell one of the old tales once more and prodded him to tell me the "prune rod" story. He did so, as well as he'd ever told it—about his father's belief (when Sparse was eight years old) in the health-giving properties of prunes, the deal struck to eat twenty-five prunes for a nickel (with a limit of fifty per week), the rod eventually bought from the proceeds of this worthwhile activity—and then he produced the huge hickory club itself.

Like that hickory "prune" rod, brilliantly waxed and protected after eighty-two years, better than it had ever been or deserved to be, whatever Sparse touched became richer, finer. A friend's prose, a lunch at which he unfolded one of his inimitable stories, a day on the Willowemoc with him, a thousand lives he touched, a memory, an Anglers Club *Bulletin* edited with his discerning eye, an event he'd lived or carefully researched—all were brighter, more memorable for his ministrations. He could make us laugh with a fantastic story about a fifty-pound brown trout that devoured pieces of bread soaked in scotch and make us cry when we read "A Drink of Water." Nearly blind in one eye and with only 20 percent vision in the other, he was still the most meticulous proofreader I ever knew and always the firmest, most exacting critic. He saw more than any of us, remembered it precisely, and then crafted his words with choicest care. The trout were not taking, but a boy along on the trip "rose to chocolate bars all day long"; some of the finest fishing is in print; he always wanted to fish "not better but more." His counsel and encouragement to a hundred lesser writers, some quite famous, has yet to be chronicled properly, and his own prose remains a constant lesson.

The day after his first growl, he gave me "Murder" to use, and he kept giving for fifteen years—a score of unforgettable moments and a piece of his heart. With a roar like a werewolf, Sparse could not hide that he was really mostly a gentleman and a lamb. He practiced a code from another, nearly forgotten time, and it included strong doses of honor, steadfastness, loyalty, dignity, backbone, pride, the art of making truly careful sentences and the art of being a gentleman, and love.

He had been a reporter for the *Wall Street Journal* and then, until several years ago, a stockholder-relations counsel; he went to work every day, well into his eighties. In his last years, old age did its best to ravage him. The doctors rummaged around inside him and did their worst; at times he had tubes attached here and there and less than a full complement of parts. But most painful must have been the loss of his beautiful and astonishing memory, which no doubt had helped him become the debating champion of New York State long before the First World War. Hoagy, who saw him a couple of weeks shy of his ninety-first birthday, reported that the only gift he wanted was "the ticket out of here." He died on Veterans Day and would have liked that.

Everyone who knew Sparse will miss him sorely—not because he was always an easy man, which he wasn't, but because there is not a chance, buster, that we shall see your likes again. He imputed to the world of fly fishing, which he loved deeply, a sense of character and tradition and wit; he saw it as a human activity, full of wonder and excitement, far beyond the mere catching of fish—an activity that enlivened the heart and sparked the imagination. It had the power to bring out the best in men—and some of the worst. He told us about the stupidity of much high-pressured "sport" and the fun we might have on our fishless days. He was far more than what he'd admit to: "Merely a good reporter, bub." He was a superb writer, who will be read a hundred years from now, and a great-hearted, humorous, and perfectly remarkable man.

It is winter now and I delight to imagine us finally off someplace in the snow, sitting on a log, puffing at pipes whose ashes sizzle and sink as they hit the snow. "Why don't you just tell me that 'fly in the nose' story one more time, old friend," I say. He grunts and chuckles and screws up his face, then says, "Well, it was an early Sunday morning in Pennsylvania, buster, and..." And my face keeps aching from laughter and I don't notice the cold, and finally, like some great chord, the senior member of the Parkside Anglers Association gets knocked nearly senseless for the second time.

SPLAT, SPLAT

It's winter now and the city is a mess. There are ruts of dirty ice and patches of gray slush everywhere. From my window I can see half a dozen people, hunched over and nearly hidden in their overcoats, walking briskly and breathing smoke. Wet snow flurries changed this afternoon to rain and sleet. This morning I got a letter from Craig Mathews in West Yellowstone and have read it over three times. He'd been midge fishing on the lower Madison and had taken three good rainbows; in the upper right-hand corner he always notes the weather: "clear, *very* cold, −32 degrees; heavy snows expected." I could be forced to pass up an opportunity to midge fish in that. I feel cozy in my living room, left to the bright fire, the splat of sleet and heavy raindrops against the panes, and my memories.

Mostly, I have been remembering a couple of weeks I spent in Montana last summer. As usual, I'd gone out bone tired and had

holed up where I could be alone, except that my old friend Les
Ackerman happened to be holed up there, too, which proved
okay because he knew immediately what I wanted and bent his
usual routine to those needs. Les doesn't look like a lunatic. From
a distance you might take him to be your average fly-fishing enthusiast, looking ten years younger than he is. But he was in the
ski troops during the war, and though he's ten years older than
me, he could pass for ten younger. He fishes every day of the
season and he fishes with astonishing vigor and passion. He's a
fearless wader and a fright to try to follow. He cranked the engine
down for the puffing likes of me and said, "I have all autumn;
you're here for a week or so."

Mostly we explored nearby creeks and rivers for a few hours
every morning. It was leisurely fishing, mostly; we were not particularly after big fish, though we raised a few; we were not after
difficult fishing, though some of it was demanding. We fished the
Gallatin a lot, which was nearby, and the Madison, which was a
bit farther, and some odd little no-name brooks, some of which
he'd fished before, some of which we both fished for the first time.
We passed up several invitations to fish choice rivers a hundred,
two hundred miles away, which I had come two thousand miles to
fish.

It was late August. Bright afternoons trailed brisk mornings,
the evenings had the first sweet sting of the fall, and grasshoppers
were everywhere. We kicked them up in the high grasses, they
splattered against the windshield; now and again—on a windy
afternoon—they flipped into the river and we watched them sail
downstream, kicking, in the current.

Early in the second week, when I wanted a bit more adventure, Les shoved me into one of his float tubes and we frog-kicked
around a couple of local lakes. It was the first time I'd been in one
of those contraptions and I enjoyed paddling backward, so close to
the roof of the liquid world beneath me, watching the pelicans,
Canada geese, mallards, and ospreys. Across the lake, over one of
the broad meadows, a hawk was working in long gliding swoops.
We saw a moose and a small herd of elk. On the surface of the
lake I watched a plump mayfly wriggle from its nymphal shuck and
hatch, plucked a few *Baetis* spinners out of the film, and trailed

my hand and line slowly. I picked up a couple of modest browns the second time out and a chunky rainbow, like a bright silver football, the third.

It was a pleasant, restful time, with the kind of happy, leisurely rhythms that are addictive. If I could steal a month, six weeks of fishing every year, I thought, I could blissfully live in gray New York forever—no matter that we'd been mugged this year, rents were skyrocketing, business was too busy, and you didn't step on soil from one month to the next.

But as I sit in this warm room in the midst of winter, I'd as well be here as anywhere else right now. I have my books, my papers, and this antique Underwood Standard to peck at, and the sleet is splatting merrily against the windowpanes. And I have my memories.

Most, I remember the late afternoons on the Gallatin, after I'd done my serious fishing for the day, when I went with Mari down to the meadows.

Craggy bluffs rose on the opposite side of the river, and when the sun hit them, they glowed a tawny red. Mari had begun a series of watercolors, and the forms—looming and etched against the bright blue sky, the layers of the canyon built into Vs and almost abstract, divorced from their local meaning—satisfied her very much. Thoughts of the few hours ahead always satisfied me very much as we chose a motif for the day and pulled off the highway onto a dirt and rutted road heading toward the river.

When she had set out her paper, palette, brushes, and paints and had filled an olive jar with water from the river, I'd start to fuss with my tackle. I would set out my waders to dry on top of the car (they'd begun to leak) and rig up one of my longer fly rods. Then I'd tuck a half-dozen flies into a Sucrets box, pop the thing into the top pocket of my shirt, and tramp off downriver.

I'd stay low on the bank and cast across and slightly upstream with a Sparrow, that marvelous nymph-what-have-you originated by Jack Gartside and nicely adapted by Don Kast, the fine tier and excellent Gallatin guide. If the water was deep, I'd cast a bit farther upstream, to get the fly down; when I found a shallow riffle, I'd cast across and downstream and let the fly swing in the current. The fly was fetching. Bright wild rainbows would suddenly tighten at the end of the line and jump briskly, flashes of wet silver.

When I'd gone a half-mile or more downstream—the fishing leisurely and languid enough for me to pass up lots of good water on the opposite side of the river, which I couldn't reach from my shore—I'd stop, sit on the bank with my back against a jackleg fence, in the midst of gray sagebrush and lemon-yellow cinquefoil and Indian paintbrush, change my sunglasses for a pair that would let me see the eye of a fly, and smoke a cigar. I'd smoke it very slowly.

The daily late-afternoon gusts would have come up by then, and the slant of the sun sparkled the broken water in ten thousand diamonds of light. Was that a spurt of water near the midriver rock? A grasshopper would land on my khaki pants, I'd trap it, look at it carefully, and compare it favorably to my Jay-Dave's Hopper, and then chuck the kicking thing out into the current.

This was the time I liked best. I'd tie on a #10 hopper and head slowly upstream, watching the water for fish, for likely runs. I'd try the far current if I could reach it, or the riffle where two branches of the river came together, or the eddy behind the boulder two-thirds across. The hopper would roll over on the cast and slap down on the water with a pretty little *splat*. I'd see the electric flash of a dark form in the clear river, and there would be a spurt of water and a fish would be on. How many did I catch and turn back each day on that hour's slow walk upstream? Enough. More than enough. The fish seemed to be everywhere—along the far bank, in midcurrent, behind the boulders, where the riffles became pools. I'd even fished with a short line against the near bank, casting fifteen feet directly upstream, where grasses hung over the water and the river carved caverns under the sod, and I would watch the rainbows and browns bust up out from the dark, no more than three or four feet below me, and blast the fly. The biggest fish were there, right below me, where I'd always ignored them, and on consecutive afternoons I raised but did not hook a rainbow that left me trembling.

By eight on that last night we were ready to leave. The rush of the wind stopped. I watched the water closely while Mari put away the last of her supplies. The evening caddis hatch would start in a few moments; I'd fished it twice and had done very well with a little #16 Elk Hair pattern. I'd pass that up tonight. Almost as an afterthought I caught a couple of grasshoppers in the sagebrush, tossed them in at the head of a run, and watched the two quick spurt-rises—*splat, splat*—like rain and sleet splashing against a living room window in the dead of winter.

ABOUT THE AUTHOR

Nick Lyons is the author of *Bright Rivers, Fishing Widows,* and *The Seasonable Angler* and editor of *Fisherman's Bounty.* His articles have appeared in *Harper's, The New York Times, Field & Stream, Sports Afield,* and *Rod & Reel.* He writes a regular column, "The Seasonable Angler," for *Fly Fisherman* magazine. A former professor of English, he is currently a book publisher.